ABOUT THIS BOOK

Moving to the Country is for anyone who has ever, even wistfully, considered moving from an urban to a rural area.

This book records the experiences of urban dwellers who in the 1970's and 1980's voluntarily chose to live in rural areas on less money than they had previously been earning.

This is not the typical "how to succeed" homesteading story or a country version of the power of positive thinking; rather it is a chronicle of the doubts, fears, decisions, joys, and successes of those who moved, and even of some who returned to the urban areas from which they hailed. Quotations from these migrants are used to document the experiences which they describe.

These pages provide sensitive and delightful insights into the life-affirming decisions and experiences of these former urban residents.

The knowledge that these migrants gained in the decades of the '70's and '80's may become a signpost for others in the 1990's and beyond.

Though raised in the country, the author lived in an urban area for many years before returning to the rural Ozarks ten years ago. He holds a Ph.D. degree in community development.

MOVING

TO THE

COUNTRY

MOVING

TO THE

COUNTRY

by ROBERT McGILL

Illustrated by Valarie Waldorf

White Oak Press
Reeds Spring, Mo.

MOVING
TO THE
COUNTRY

White Oak Press
P.O. Box 188
Reeds Spring, Mo. 65737

Manufactured in the United States of America
Library of Congress Card Number 86-50758
ISBN: 0-935069-17-8

ACKNOWLEDGEMENTS

The thought, research, and writing of this book have taken several years. Different people, at different periods, participated in its development. Drs. Bryan Phifer and John Keane encouraged the formation of the idea. Jim and Jane Thompson, Rex Campbell, and the late Wallace Wells encouraged and commented on the early drafts. Vicki May typed several research drafts before the work was transferred to a computer. Patsi Yarnell assisted with valuable editorial help. The late Dan Saults, Jory Sherman, who insists that writing is a disease, Edith McCall and the "Red Lion" Associates offered encouragement. My appreciation, too, to Don Littrell, Charlotte George, and Bill Elder. Finally, Frank Reuter encouraged further research and helped develop the final format. Computer assistance has been freely given by Don Shanafelt and James Morris of Database Systems, Inc. Inspiration, too, came from Chris, Heather, and Denise.

Those that I interviewed have my profound admiration and I consider them my "heroes" for what they have undertaken.

CONTENTS

PREFACE

Beginning in the late 1960's, a well-defined exodus occurred from America's urban areas. Though only a small percentage of urban residents took part in the move, their numbers were great enough that some rural areas which for years had been stagnant or declining in population began to experience population increases. These new settlers were searching for less stressful areas in which to live. In some places, such as the Ozark mountain region of Missouri and Arkansas, this increase was dramatic. The relatively cheap land prices which prevailed in the region a decade ago may have been an important factor in drawing many of these migrants to the Ozarks. The in-migrants were intent on settling down, raising families, and becoming a permanent part of community life. They chose a new style of life, for, in leaving the cities and suburbs, many left well paying jobs and economic security for a life of hard work and rural simplicity.

This book chronicles the experiences of migrants who, by moving to the Ozarks, have lowered their incomes and changed their lifestyles. Direct interviews tell of their dissatisfactions with urban life, their aspirations for country living, and their triumphs and failures. The book is also intended to serve as a guidebook for individuals who are contemplating a move to a rural area. The experiences of those who have already come can serve both to offer guidance and to forewarn.

My own experiences parallel to some extent the material covered in the book. Though I was born in the Ozarks, as a young man I was temporarily lured to the city. When I was a boy, people were moving away from the Ozarks. Towns had many vacant buildings and houses, and young people talked about jobs in the cities. A few places resembled old by-gone western ghost towns rather than settled communities. Many small towns had simply disappeared. But by the time of my return, the decline in population was reversing. The Ozarks were filling up. Opportunities existed which had not been present in my youth. More employment was available. Local colleges and universities had expanded. In a few scattered locations, retirement towns had been built. Senior citizens were moving in to enjoy the beauty of the mountains and the outdoor activities. Increased opportunities in the region prompted young people to stay. The area was experiencing a population increase. A reversal in the social life of a region had taken place, and one I had not expected.

I returned to the Ozarks as an employee of the University of Missouri Extension Service. My job, working with 4-H clubs and occasionally offering agricultural assistance, gave me the opportunity to know both old-time residents and many of the newcomers. I talked to scores of former urban dwellers about their experiences. Finally, I armed myself with a tape recorder and listened as a few in-migrants told their stories. In-depth interviews were eventually conducted with over thirty people. Without exception, those I interviewed were willing to share their experiences. I sat around kitchen tables in the morning, living rooms at night, and workshops during the afternoon. In one store I even helped wait on customers as we talked. Discussions were lively, and often it was difficult to stop. People had obviously been caught up in an exciting experience and wanted others to know what they had done. They were experimenting with how to live and using themselves as the focus of their own experiments.

One particular aspect of the interviews fascinated me. Those who were moving to the Ozarks were migrating for other than the traditional reasons: economic opportunity, jobs, and expanding community services. Their coming, at first, appeared illogical. They were lowering their incomes as they moved and were obviously experiencing major disruptions. People who came into my office at the County Extension Center spoke of the good jobs they had had in metropolitan areas and of the so-called "finer" things of life they had enjoyed. A few had obviously experienced great affluence. Yet, they were asking questions about how to build greenhouses, produce feeder pigs, grow vegetables, or tend orchards. They asked elementary questions about what to them were complicated ventures. Frequently I wondered how they could have moved with such meager information. At times it would have been easy to suggest that they return to the urban areas from which they came and make their changes in surroundings which would have been much more in keeping with their past experiences. And yet, there was a persistence about them which could not be easily dismissed. Their financial decisions were the most obvious signals they made of their intentions to change. In order to migrate many of them had knowingly and intentionally taken reductions in income, often drastic reductions. I became acquainted with a former executive whose income had dropped from $60,000 to $3,000 in one year. An airline mechanic dropped from $30,000 to $7,000. Admittedly most reductions in income were moderate--if a reduction of several thousand dollars can be called moderate. Most lowered their family incomes from $20,000 or

$30,000 down to $10,000 or $15,000. And in all cases the reductions caused apprehensions.

Not everyone stayed after the move. The experiences of some were transitory; they came, stayed a while, and left. But the largest group appeared to be those who had lowered their incomes, been in the area three, four, or five years, and were insistent that they would remain indefinitely. They had become contributing and sustaining members of the communities in which they live. They succeeded.

This book, then, is the story of the in-migrants told in their own words. It is a testimony of a choice many people have made to simplify their lives. It is not a romantic tale. Those considering a similar move should read the text carefully and be prepared to deal with many unanticipated problems.

Perhaps, too, this is the story of a new breed of social pioneers. There have been times in the recent past when many people in this country were forced to take reductions in income. Those times may come again. And if they do, it may be invaluable to those who are fired, laid off, or lose pensions to discover the experiences of others who have "made-do" with less money. In that case the experiences of these people may serve as a model for those who are forced to take mandatory as well as voluntary cuts in income, whether they live in urban or rural areas. If a major recession or depression again appears, a guiding path may have already been marked by these pioneers.

CHAPTER I

THE MIGRANTS

Twenty years ago I was teaching college in a medium--sized town in the Midwest. One of my students, a friend, told me about a decision he had made a few years earlier. Bill said he had previously lived in a large metropolitan area. One morning, as he was driving to work on a crowded freeway, he began thinking about his job on an airplane manufacturing line. He told me that he just couldn't go there and put all those bolts, nuts, and little pieces of metal in place any more. He exited the freeway, sped home, talked his wife into leaving, loaded their belongings in the family car, and moved. Bill wanted a drastic change in his life. He believed a simpler life was possible by living in a rural area and so he purchased a small farm in central Missouri which was suitable for organic farming. The two of us spent many hours talking about his hopes, desires, and possibilities for success. Bill moved from his farm several years later and I lost contact with him, but our conversations continued to intrigue me.

Eventually I learned that Bill did what others were talking about doing. Even twenty years ago I knew co-workers who had moments when they would say, "If I could I'd leave this place and..." Perhaps such statements were a normal reaction to frustration, but a few friends who seemed quite stable with their employment, acquaintances, and surroundings told me that they had developed "escape plans" to move to the country just in case the time ever came when they might need them. Over the years I realized that many people in this nation did activate their "escape plans." Bill, it became evident, was only one of the first in what became a migration of people who moved from urban to rural areas. Those who did move made more than just a change in geography. They experienced a difficult transition. They purposely changed their lifestyles.

We know that difficult moves and migrations have their historical precedence in the earliest traditions of the nation. This country, as we are all aware, was formed by wave after wave of emigrants traveling from Europe, by the forced migrations of slaves from Africa, and by the influx of Asians on the West Coast. Today the Spanish-speaking people, often at great personal risk, move across the southern borders into the United States. The stories which have evolved about those who have participated in migrations are fascinating to most of us. We are inspired by the saga of a forlorn immigrant arriving by ship in New York Harbor, a family traveling west in a covered wagon, a black sharecropper's wife deciding to take her family to a northern city, or an illegal alien slipping across the southern border looking for better working conditions. Such movements tell of heroism, courage, error, and occasional tragedy, and as such become the raw material from which novels are written, movies produced, and television series created.

Such stories enthrall not just because they happen, but because most people believe that the aspirations which motivate migrants are the same values and beliefs which are common throughout society. After all, all but a very few of us share a common heritage with these migrants. Most of our forebearers migrated to the United States to better themselves or their children. The risks they took meant they desired greater freedom, more goods, better housing, or increased educational opportunity.

In the migration described in this book, those who moved also wanted to better their own lives. This migration, which crested during the 1970's, seemed to have its roots in the industrial areas of the north and east. People left those metropolitan areas and moved to the south and southwestern parts of the United States. Many who made the move simply shifted their residences to other cities. Presumably they found employment opportunities similar to what they had had. But one of the surprises of this migration was that the rural regions, or non-metropolitan areas as the census calls them, in the United States increased in population faster than did urban areas. This was particularly true in the south and southwest.[1] Not since the founding of the nation had this happened.

Those who relocated into the Ozarks were a part of this movement. The influx reversed a population trend which had existed in the region for over seventy years. The fascinating heritage of the Ozarks undoubtedly lured some to settle within its borders.

The Ozarks are often defined as both a geographical and social area. As a geographical area, the region extends from the Mississippi River westward to the prairies of Kansas, and from the Missouri River on the north to the Arkansas River on the south. The landscape is old with a rough terrain of deep valleys rather than protruding mountains, and is rich in beautiful scenery of natural hardwood forests, meandering streams, and man-made impoundments.

The cultural heritage of the Ozarks began with the first settlers. Since the terrain of the Ozarks is so rugged, many of these first settlers arrived by the waterways which surround the area. The first pioneers traveled down the Mississippi River and settled on its banks in the early 1700's, well before the nation was formed. But the dominant influence on the early culture came from the Scotch-Irish of Tennessee and Kentucky who in the first half of the 1800's explored many of the remote rivers and streams in the interior. They normally avoided the few settlements which already existed and settled in the remote valleys of the region. The Scotch-Irish were known to be hardy folks. They were industrious, independent, and self-sufficient--qualities to which the present day in-migrants also aspire. These early settlers gave the Ozarks much of its early cultural heritage and were, perhaps, the forerunners of the legendary "hillbillys" of the area.[2]

These early settlers were followed, after the civil war, by a flood of other immigrants. Towns by the name of Versailles, Rosati, Freistatt, and Pulaskifield dot the landscape and attest to the fact that ethnic groups arrived from France, Italy, Germany, Poland, and other European nations to inhabit the region. These groups homesteaded small farms and logged the bountiful forests. But this period of growth was short lived. Young people wanted to leave the area as quickly as their parents brought them in. The exodus from rural areas which occurred elsewhere in the nation dominated the Ozarks. Most young people were lured by the excitement of city life. To them urban areas promised jobs, money, leisure time, and adventure. This exodus was so severe that most Ozark counties had a higher population in 1900 than they did seventy years later in 1970. Normally, only those few Ozark counties that contained large towns or small cities retained their population and grew. The rural areas experienced a downward population spiral that lasted for more than half a century.

However, by the 1930's the governmental and community services which would eventually help attract the wave of migrants in the 1970's, began to appear in the Ozarks. Over the next three decades farms were mechanized, schools consolidated, and electrical lines, telephone services, and good roads constructed. Meanwhile, in the Ozark towns and cities industry grew steadily, commerce expanded, and good colleges and universities were established and fostered. In a few places, as in Stone County, Missouri, where I reside, major lakes were built which prompted the development of a tourist industry and retirement settlements.[3]

In spite of this progress, the population increase in the Ozarks during the 1970's was unexpected. Some of the increase came when young people in the area found that a new alternative--to stay--became available to them. But a more forceful change loomed on the horizon. Outsiders found the Ozarks. A cross section of American society began to arrive. Retirement aged residents were among the first permanent arrivals. These retirees moved into lakeside cottages, established themselves on small farms, or purchased homes in the new retirement villages which had been built to accommodate them. Families with young or middle-aged wage earners, who needed employment and wanted to maintain their previous standard of living, arrived. They found an assortment of jobs in the tourist industry or service trades. A few established their own businesses. They practiced their old skills as electricians, builders, or merchants. Some had to drive long distances each day to employment in the larger towns. Many, regardless of their occupations, settled on small plots of land and worked at part-time and temporary jobs while also farming their small acreages.[4]

But some of the people coming into the University Extension Office seeking information about small farm agriculture and the Ozarks had not maintained their previous incomes. These people knowingly and intentionally lowered their incomes by moving into the Ozark hills. They methodically and persistently insisted that they could learn the skills of living with less money instead of more and, thereby, increase the quality of their lives.

The conversations that I had with them indicated that they were embarking on a much different way of living than they had previously pursued. I wanted to learn more about their decisions, what prompted them to move to the area, the experiences they encountered, and the eventual results of their efforts.

Almost immediately, the first common theme emerged. Before they moved, almost all had experienced a period when they had been unhappy. They had become disenchanted with the urban areas in which they found themselves. Time after time they poured forth with unpleasant stories about life before the transition.

Sometimes a seemingly small event triggered the desire to move. One former teacher trembled and shouted in the serenity of his own home when he related the events leading to his decision to move.

Albert: Do you know what finally did it for me? It was because of the administrators. I enjoyed teaching. I'd go to class and teach and really get involved with my students. They were learning. I was a good teacher. Then, I'd get out of class and go to my office and there would be a silly memo from an administrator telling me to do something that in no way was related to teaching. Often, the rules they handed down were detrimental to good instruction, and I knew it. That's what I found frustrating and confusing. It made me want to quit and find something better.

A dichotomy had developed in this man's life, as it had in so many others. These people were unhappy. They wanted peace, love, and harmony within, but when they searched themselves they found frustration, anxiety, and uncertainty. Most believed that the urban area was at least partially responsible for this rift and if they could only move to a rural area where life was simpler they could more easily take control of the major decisions which affected them. A move to the rural area, they believed, would help correct the ills of their lives.

Sometimes the decisions to move were extremely abrupt. This man described a decision he had made seven years earlier:

Tom: I went back to Kansas City and picked up the boys. I left graduate school even though I felt the responsible thing to do was to be in graduate school and go ahead and get the degree. But, one day I found I could get custody of the boys and so I made a decision to go to Arkansas and start a small business. It was a greedy thing--get my boys and go to Arkansas. I knew I was going to be poor. But I wanted to get away. I'd been in college five years. My whole life up to that point had been doing what I needed to do--doing what I was supposed to do. I was just sick of waiting. It was time I did something for myself. It seemed my whole life had been a matter of preparation. So I went to Arkansas.

Once people moved, they sought to put wholeness and completeness back into their lives. A change, not only in residence and employment but also in thoughts and values, was involved. Even those who succeeded normally took several years to pass from their disillusionment with urban life through the moves and adjustments in the rural environment before stability again took hold. Everyone's experiences were different, but, the significant events were often similar. Predictable and definable stages emerged. And, it was encouraging to me to realize early in the study that most found the experience rewarding.

Here is a typical statement which reflects the new-found serenity of the rural area. Notice that this statement was made by the same person who made the quotation directly above.

Tom: I don't need anything to fill my hours up now. I have so many projects lined up, so many things to do and want to do, that I'm about five years behind. I work--or play--whatever you want to call it, about eighteen hours a day, seven days a week, and don't have time to get done half of what I want to do--let alone what I need to do. I've always been three or four years behind with projects. Basically, I want to build things.

Bob: You have that well defined, don't you?

Tom: Yes, I know pretty well what I'm doing and where I'm going. There's not much doubt in my mind about where I want to end up.

Bob: Do you consider yourself fortunate?

Tom: Oh, I'm real lucky. I wouldn't trade spots with anyone I know. No, I can't think of anyone I'd trade places with. There's nobody I envy.

CHAPTER II

DOUBTS AND DISCONTENTS

Almost everyone I interviewed revealed that there was a time when each had become disenchanted with urban living. The doubts had begun as small concerns but progressed for months and even years until they became agonizing distractions. Most felt they had lost purpose in life. They had little control over their own actions and were participating in events which were devoid of meaning. They felt helpless and wondered if they could be sustained in urban areas.

This man recalled his helplessness one day as we were sitting in his shop. He was gesturing wildly and speaking vigorously as he told of his past fears of losing his identity and becoming an inseparable part of a crowd.

Martin: I moved up into the mountains in a large estate in California. I was 20 miles from San Jose and 45 to 50 miles from San Francisco. I was still right in the same general area as the city, but it was peaceful, quiet. And, it contributed to my corruption. I saw all those people go to work every morning. I would drive down this highway into the city. It was just incredibly beautiful--big trees, green and lovely, and very few cars. Traffic would pick up as I got closer and closer to the city. And the speed would pick up. Everybody would be going 50 to 55 down the

> hill and when they hit the flat land they would put their foot on the accelerator. They would increase to 70 or 75. Every day at the same spot on the freeway they would slam on their brakes. At the same spot! There would be a half-dozen fenderbenders! Every day! It didn't change! It was like people caught in a trap. You wind them up and they do the same thing. I know I sound just like a lot of people but they came to the same conclusion. I wanted to scream, 'Let me out of here! This is insane!' Others may have thought I was crazy. I thought they were crazy.

Such intense sentiments developed slowly and were normally the culmination of long periods of doubts and discouragement. Usually people had trouble identifying exactly when they first contemplated moving to rural areas. Almost no one talked of dramatic and sudden inspirations. Rather, the reverse was true. The transition initially began with apathy, discontent, and frustration about concerns which had little immediate affect on their everyday lives. These first doubts could only be identified in vague and nebulous ways, but they would not cease. They broke through to consciousness during moments of leisure, relaxation, or intellectual discussions.

The Normal Doubt

Often the first doubts which so many people recalled dealt with events far beyond their personal control. Nevertheless, they felt that the actions and decisions of others who controlled them impinged on their own lives. Many times these first doubts dealt with national and international issues. Often frustrations were approached as ethical or philosophical issues. For example, several people expressed the realization that they lived in the midst of a society which produced more goods for more people than had any other in the history of the world. They knew people lived longer, received better medical treatment, attended better schools, and communicated with more sophisticated equipment than had ever existed before. It was because of these advantages that many had participated so vigorously in society. They had been intent on educating themselves, holding good jobs, working industriously in their employment, and participating in community and neighborhood life. They wanted a good life for themselves, their families, and their children, and had expected their efforts to be adequately rewarded.

Nevertheless, their doubts surfaced. The future migrants began to point out inconsistencies and inequities in society. These same people were troubled that the nations of the world were divided between those who had plenty and those with little; that there was poverty in the midst of affluent cities; that wealth was concentrated in cities and suburbs; that government regulations often strangled small businessmen who were struggling to establish new enterprises; that the elderly often had only subsistence level incomes; and that crime endangered the lives of urban residents. Those who moved questioned the extent to which they could participate in a society which allowed these conditions to exist.

The doubts which this woman experienced years ago when she was just beginning her career led directly to her decision to move to the country. They dealt with international issues.

Lisa: The Hungarian Revolution started it all for me. I know it happened years ago. But, we promised those

> people that if they revolted, we would help them. We told them we would come to their rescue. And those people believed us. They stood up to the Communists, and we didn't help those poor people. We made them face the Russian tanks all by themselves. When we did that I thought, 'Who can you believe?' From then on I began to question almost everything. That questioning led directly to where I am now.

For a while it seemed to some that the discontentments and doubts had a life of their own, as might a fantasy, dream, or fervent desire, for the doubts slowly intensified and as they did so they redirected themselves. Instead of remaining focused on international or national events, they developed into issues and concerns which were immediate and emotional. People turned their attentions to everyday events which restricted and limited them. Employment problems were measured in terms of bureaucratic entanglements, drudgery at the office, and conflicts with the boss, while political ineptness became the length of time it took to build or repair freeways and the inconvenience of driving to and from work. They translated theft and crime into the amount of taxes they had to pay to maintain police forces, establish order, and repair vandalism. And, perhaps above all, almost everyone had to hurry from one activity to another in order to meet all the commitments they had made to family, friends, and acquaintances. Because they lived in urban areas, they saw this crowded environment as responsible for many of their problems.

Here's another typical story about society infringing on the lives of children. A mother who was concerned about her three high school age children told about one of her reasons for moving.

Hester: The related drug culture was part of our decision to come here. It got to the point where they were selling drugs in our high schools. We didn't think that was right--not necessarily because of the marijuana but because of the lawless effect it had on the children. It was teaching children to follow new rules. They were prone enough to do that anyway. Then, too, there was no supervision at school. The school monitors looked the other way in the halls. They didn't have the energy to combat drugs. They might jump onto one kid one day and another the next. But they can't jump onto 60 or 70 kids a week.

Many city dwellers feared that not only had they lost control of events around them, but that they would never be able to regain control. Society seemed to be too disjointed. Many concluded this particularly when they viewed their own dependence on the national and local economic scene. They believed that the money economy would collapse.

An often repeated statement was that a financial collapse would definitely occur in the nation and the world. A young, hard-working father made this statement one day while we were drinking coffee in a local restaurant.

Don: We're kidding ourselves. Our nation is borrowing all of this money and there's no way to pay it back. Our national debt is horrible, and so is the debt of other countries. We're borrowing time instead of money. A day of reckoning will come, and things will be bad when that happens. One way or the other, we'll pay it back. I've heard a lot of people talk about the depression of the thirties. I think there's a good chance things will be even worse than that when the economy collapses.

But people expressed discontent with more than just social, political, and financial conditions. Other doubts were personal in nature. Those who eventually moved questioned themselves, their place in society, and what had led them to be where they were. They were, after all, active participants in society and had made at least some of the decisions which led to their dissatisfaction. If life was not what they wanted it to be, who could they blame but themselves? If, they reasoned, their lives were to have meaning, they had to take some responsibility for the situations in which they found themselves.

Instead of looking outward to find reasons for their apprehensions, people began looking inward for the causes of their restlessness. This inward search began in a nebulous way when people found themselves indecisive. They weren't sure what they wanted. They only knew that to continue as they were would be unsatisfactory. Often, because employment was extremely important, dissatisfaction was expressed with work. Many times people talked about the need for another kind of employment.

Dissatisfaction with work prompted people to question their own decisions to remain where they were. Many believed their employment contributed to their unhappiness. This statement is similar to many I heard.

Jack: Oh yes, I was making good money. My house was almost paid for. I worked hard. I punched the clock and took $500.00 home every week. Oh yes, I was well trained, too. When I left, it took a year to train the person who took my place. My pension would have been good.

I'd have gotten ahead if I'd stayed. I was there almost ten years. I had everything but peace of mind. There were no windows at work and I was a country boy, originally. I just needed to get out. We had a neighbor who drove 50 miles to work one way each day. He was a carpenter. When he got home, he worked a second job. He worked all the time. On the week-end he went fishing by himself. His wife didn't work. I don't know what she did. But they were never together. Now, that kind of life is destructive. That's not living. I used to talk to him about that.

Others believed they were over-committed to family, friends, school, and church. Many times they could not adequately cope with all of the demands that were being placed on them. Instead of being satisfied with the efforts they did make, they became disturbed at themselves for not accomplishing more. These were often highly skilled people who had been ambitious and had successfully undertaken many responsibilities. But the pressures of daily living were breeding discontent and unhappiness. Often they lacked the ability to express their emotions in any satisfactory way, turning their anger inward and blaming themselves even when the ineptness of others was causing their frustration.

Inevitably, they spoke about their lives in terms of tension, stress, and anxiety. Many were burned out. They lost interest in what had previously been important to them. Almost everyone reported that to some extent they were nervous, forgetful, or preoccupied. Some smoked too much, drank too much, or were impatient with family and friends. Most believed that these mannerisms signaled the degree to which their daily activities were out of step with what they wanted them to be. They began to notice how they had ceased to grow as individuals and had begun to wither.

This gregarious young couple could easily pinpoint the reasons for their decision to move.

Bob: Joan, what made you decide to leave?

Joan: [Joan turned to her husband, pointed, and laughed.] He did. I was working two jobs when we met. I was a waitress at night and he would come in and get coffee and soon we were going together. We vacationed together and had a lot of fun but he talked to me about what I was doing--and somehow I knew there was a better way. Then I got a job as a welfare worker--doing things to help other people. I worked with children. But you know, I couldn't do anything. I couldn't coordinate all the services that they needed.

Bill: She was a good one, too. She was aggressive. She stood up for the children. But no one appreciated her. She gave too much of herself. They didn't like that.

Joan: That's right. That's what he told me. Other people went by the book. I just did what was needed. I'd bring a bus load of kids to my house to look at the garden or, if a day care mother was good with children but her fire extinguisher was in the wrong place, I'd stand up for her. And, I wouldn't stand for child abuse, either. Others would just turn their heads and walk away; but I wouldn't. I stood up for the kids, reported parents, and saw to it that services were worked out. Everyone was coming to me with problems, and I fought back when others wouldn't. I was an advocate and pretty soon I was running the place--even though I was only an administrative assistant. I was doing everything, but I wasn't having any results. There were too many kids who still had problems. I was getting cynical and burned out. When I quit, everyone got mad. They wouldn't talk to me. I had told them to fight back--and now I was quitting. They always had a party when someone left, but not for me. They were polite, but they were mad. I couldn't make them understand I was not mad at them. I was doing it for me.

At other times thoughts of eventual retirement led to self-doubts. People anticipated the end of their working careers and wondered if they could continue with what they were doing until then. Most who eventually moved had found their previous employment a drudgery, and they were aware how many hours a day they spent at their places of work. They had wondered if they should wait to find satisfaction and peace of mind. Perhaps an illness, misfortune, tragedy, or death would befall them prior to retirement. They often felt they were giving up too much in return for any long-term security they might be gaining.

This statement was made prior to a community meeting which Lester and I both attended. He was extremely intent and concise in his reasoning.

Lester: I was working for the utility company and was up for a promotion. I'd been at it for ten years. I had to decide to accept the promotion and do more of the same or get out. I had a chance to get my money from the retirement fund and so I did. We took the money and came down here. You don't know what's going to happen if you wait until you retire to do what you like. You may lose your health, die, or change your mind. I wanted to move while we still had the time and health to enjoy life. So, we moved.

Many times people talked about death. Several told me about friends, often energetic young people in their thirties, who had suffered heart attacks and died. A few recounted the suicides of acquaintances. Nor was it unusual for someone to tell of their own fleeting thoughts of suicide. Often, I felt, people had confronted their mortality. The knowledge that they would surely die helped them search for another way to live. To many who were already considering changes, this realization added an urgency to complete the decision. No one wanted a future that would be a continuation of their unhappy past and eventually to die with unfulfilled dreams.

Still another man reflected upon the urgency and depth of his decision to leave.

Cliff: I had two good friends who died over a period of a couple of years. They had heart attacks and were gone--just like that! Then, another man down the street committed suicide. He seemed to be well adjusted. He had a wife and family. Pressures just got to him. He left a note at home saying he just couldn't keep up with everything people wanted from him. So, he left everything. I thought about that a lot. I would have ended up like that. I decided there was a better way to live. It made me want to move.

Doubts affected all people who eventually moved. Normally the discontentment grew over a period of months and even years. For most these doubts were not constant but surfaced intermittently, the way bubbles in a slowly heating pan of water ascend. As people questioned conditions under which they were living, they began to wonder if they had to continue to live in a way that was so void of meaning. Most carried on their daily activities while they contemplated what was wrong. And yet, their disenchantments were great enough to prompt them to consider major changes in lifestyles. They wanted to gain control of more of their own activities and wondered if a change might not help them simplify their lives.

Collapsed Lifestyle

Occasionally a few people related experiences which were traumatic enough to have caused disastrous disruptions to their lives. These individuals could not carry on minimal daily activities. They could not follow daily routines nor make adequate plans for altering what they could not accomplish. Usually, against their own wishes, others had to attend to and care for them and often made decisions about what they could and should do. They were incapable of directing their own lives. Their lifestyles had collapsed.

The collapses were often physical. Sometimes either accidents or illnesses had impaired people's ability to work, play, and enjoy life. Those so affected felt that the misfortune was connected to outside pressures which caused tension or stress. The collapses added an immediacy to the need for changes, while also immeasurably complicating them.

Vern related to me how he had radically changed his life after suffering a heart attack. We were sitting in a new home that, with great physical difficulty, he had recently completed.

Bob: How long after you had your first heart attack was it before you actually moved? Did you go back to work for a while?

Vern: I worked for almost four years after I had my heart attack. I was off work for almost four months with the heart attack. The doctors didn't want me to go back to my old job because it was so hard. I always felt like I was an average American citizen. I couldn't afford to quit that job and start out somewhere else on the bottom because it took every penny I was earning to make ends meet. There was no way I could start out at lower wages again. This is how we were always trapped. I needed every penny I could earn to make ends meet and pay taxes on our house--just to live. That's all there was to it. It was just that expensive.

Bob: What finally made you decide to leave?

Vern: My health was slipping again. I wasn't feeling good. I felt like I was just slowly skidding back to the same shape I had been in. There was just one thing to do and that was to move. There was no sense in quitting that job and looking for something different in the area. That wasn't the answer because we still lived in the same environment. We still paid the same taxes. We decided there was only one way to get away from it. That was to completely move out of the area. The pace of living was just crazy there. I always had two or three jobs. I had one full-time job and always at least one part-time job. The taxes on our house were a thousand dollars a year! This was fourteen years ago. We just couldn't make ends meet. My wife couldn't go to work. We had four children.

It would have been several years before she would have been free to work. It was just an endless struggle. We were glad to get out.

Bob: And you were working how many hours a day then?

Vern: I ended up with a heart attack and the doctors figured I was working between 70 and 80 hours a week. I couldn't see where it would get any better. I was making good money.

Others suffered emotional collapses. Simultaneously they had major doubts about themselves and the urban areas. They could not find any incentives in their daily routines, friendships, or employment. They could no longer distinguish between what they liked or disliked; nor did they know what excited, disappointed, inspired, or bored them. They had become lethargic and stripped of almost all emotion. And, they could not stimulate themselves. For, when they attempted to give direction to their own lives, they encountered only their own ambivalence. Their uniqueness as individuals had vanished and their identity was lost.

For those few who suffered this complete collapse, the period of doubt was pivotal for continuing life itself. The confusion which reigned in their lives made any decision exceedingly difficult. Yet, often the reactions they could muster to events around them were repugnant even to themselves. They told of smoking excessively, drinking much too much, and becoming habitual drug users. But stimulants succeeded only in consuming any minimal strength which they had. Several people admitted seriously contemplating suicide. They had to decide between extinguishing themselves and finding an alternative which would allow them to accept life.

These people found within themselves a gigantic cleavage between what they were and what they wanted to become. Some believed it to be an almost unbridgeable chasm. Perhaps it resembled a void. And, when they made meager attempts at placing meaning back into their lives, they could only stir up unexpected surges of anger, hostility, and anxiety. Though such efforts reintroduced emotion to their lives, people were perplexed by their feelings. The confusion enhanced the doubts which they were already experiencing.

This former executive had been an assistant to the president of a large company. He had a sudden heart attack followed by a dependency on a prescribed drug and an inability to perform any work. He and his wife describe the decision to move and the traumatic period which followed.

Mike: I tried doing work five administrative steps below where I had previously worked. I couldn't do that. I would function bright for maybe a half an hour and then I would start throwing things. I even dropped to a job one step above file clerk. I think the fact that I was trying to work so low damaged my concentration. I was just lost. I couldn't function very well. I just had to get out and function somewhere else.

Bob: You thought and talked quite a bit about the move?

Denise: Yes, we fought and cried and had all kinds of scenes about it. He came back here in March to buy the place. He wasn't going to come back to New Jersey at all.

Mike: Oh, I was too.

Denise: Well, you told me you weren't. You said you were going to stay here. Of course, he doesn't remember a lot because he was on Valium for quite a while after his heart attack. He doesn't remember a great deal of what was said or done or anything. Those months! I don't know! How long was it? A year?

Mike: I was on it two years. I tried working for about three months.

Denise: Four months. You went back to work in June.

Mike: I did. Well, they finally fired me. They finally said, 'Hey, you can't do it.'

Such trauma had a resounding impact. It produced even more fear, anger, and hostility. Those who felt it wondered where it had come from. They questioned the reasons for its intensity. Some thought it was because they had dreamed too many dreams, wanted too much, and had reached out too far. They had been in too big a hurry to get where they were going and so had never achieved the goals which they had set for themselves. Often they found they were caught in the trap of aspiring to goals and dreams other people had set for them. Daily routines were designed to fulfill the expectations of others. They had never allowed themselves the relaxation, leisure, and enjoyment which let the emotions of loving, giving, and caring to grow. They had failed to establish satisfying lifestyles. And they were angry.

Their anger was turned both inward and outward. Outward as they reflected on their association with others. They were angry with everything and everyone who put stress on their lives, including families and spouses, employers, and neighbors. They resented all of the commitments they had made. They felt they were at the mercy of others who made unwarranted demands on their time. Others, they believed, had caused them to lose control of their lives.

At other times the same anger was turned inwards. It was as if those who were so disturbed could remember all the times in the past when they had allowed others to dominate, manipulate, or control them. Such pressures had stunted their growth, and they now had difficulty giving directions to their lives. They had allowed others to dominate, and they were angry--at themselves.

This bright, articulate, and sensitive lady went straight to the heart of the matter when she stated what several others also told me.

Barbara: I did things right in my life. I went to school. I studied hard and I made good grades. Then I got married and was a good wife. I supported and helped my husband. We worked hard at our business. And, there were times when we made money. But, I began to realize that my dreams were not being fulfilled. I was doing everything everyone else wanted me to do, and there wasn't time or money left over for what I wanted to do. So, I worked harder and faster, but we didn't make more money and I didn't have any more time. People just depended on me more to do the things they wanted me to do. I began to blame myself. Why wasn't I happier, more satisfied? It was terrible for me to learn that I couldn't accomplish everything.

The emergence of anger began to fill the void which existed within. It was a starting point on a journey to self-potential. It was as if their doubts overlapped with their desire to develop potential. Doubt had become a foundation for change. For through anger people discovered the depths to which their emotions could run. Anger was the beginning of wave after wave of emotions and moods which welled up within them. The mind seemed to have been dwarfed and thwarted in the tender and caring parts of its domain, and its attempts to develop and rectify this imbalance were now breaking through. The mind, just as the body within which it resided, was reaffirming that it, too, demanded proper attention.

Almost everyone identified moments when they felt their lifestyles had nearly collapsed. For most these moments passed quickly, and they were again in control of their lives. But for these few, obviously, the breakdown lingered for much longer--sometimes for years. Often these were the migrants who moved quickly and with little forethought. Their very survival depended on their ability to change. The severe doubts they experienced were beneficial, perhaps, at least to the extent that they suffered more than others and had, therefore, experienced more than most. Their introspection was greater, their understanding more complete, and their ability to relate was accomplished with greater compassion.

STOP
DETOUR
REAL ESTATE
COUNTRY LIFE

CHAPTER III

POTENTIAL AND POSSIBILITIES

Eventually the period of doubting passed. But it had been constructive because wherever the doubt had existed, new vistas opened. Doubts transformed the troublesome feelings about life into questioning, searching, and examination. New alternatives and possibilities began to develop, and significant changes were considered.

Potential was the other side of the dichotomy. And, like the doubt which had released it, this potential also emerged from the unconscious. People began to experience dreams, fantasies, and new aspirations. Often in the beginning, these dreams and desires were a chaotic mixture of possibilities which later had to be arranged into a comprehensible pattern. At first people just wanted change. They daydreamed about traveling, starting their own businesses, living closer to relatives, or residing on farms. Simultaneously, they saw a need to transform themselves. They envisioned themselves as freer, happier, and more expressive individuals. They discovered that many of the hopes and dreams which they had held in abeyance for years, or even considered detrimental, were now a part of their active imaginations. But more important, they were now considering these aspirations in new and different ways. They began to believe that, contrary to their past beliefs, they could build their futures on these dreams.

Considering a move to the country was not easy. At times the visions which many had of their future seemed so real that they felt they could reach out and easily take hold of them. At other times almost everyone saw stumbling blocks at every turn and believed that so much change was required to reach their visions that the effort to achieve them would be almost impossible. They spent hours discussing, examining, and investigating all that was involved in moving to rural areas--and changing lifestyles. A sorting process to distinguish the possible from the impractical, the good ideas from the unworkable, and the desirable from the unachievable was necessary. In succession it was fun, enjoyable, frustrating, perplexing, and gratifying.

Initially there were two concerns which people faced. They wondered, first, where they might move. Nearly everyone wanted to own some land. It was as if there was something magic and romantic about owning a piece of land and being able to cultivate it to produce the fruits of one's own labor.

> *This wife had the thought of a farm embedded in her mind from childhood.*
>
> Marge: I grew up dreaming of living on a farm. I always wanted to do that. My parents and I would take vacations to up-state New York and always traveled through the farmlands. I liked to look out the windows and see the countryside. It was beautiful.

But owning land was only part of this concern. Since so many felt that their lives were being restricted by the urban areas in which they lived, they wanted to locate where the pace of life was slower, fewer legal and governmental restrictions existed, and individual initiative was regarded as a virtue. Such areas, they felt, would also have established traditions of self-reliance.

Another wife explained the criteria she and her ecology-conscious husband looked for in choosing a place to live.

Helen: We were very careful in choosing the place we wanted to live. We're very ecology conscious. We looked for a place where the air was clean and the water pure. We wanted to raise most of our own food so we needed garden space, and we didn't want too many people around us. No close neighbors for us!

The other issue which confronted almost everyone was the amount of money they would need in a rural area. Most were willing to live on less money, but moving, buying land, caring for a family, and enjoying some of the conveniences of life would not be cheap. Most assumed that living in a rural area would be cheaper than urban living, but by how much they were not certain.

This led them to search for ways in which they might support themselves. Even though they were interested in living on small farms, most realized they did not have the skills for farming. These skills would need to be developed after the move, so they considered several possibilities for securing an income. Most examined their jobs to determine if similar employment skills were needed in rural areas. They searched through skills and hobbies to see what other businesses might be developed. Others considered purchasing an existing small business or even beginning their own. They were resourceful in their investigations.

After careful consideration this young couple decided they could not live solely from the land they purchased.

Nadine: I had the great American dream. We were going to have goats for milk and cheese, chickens for eggs, and raise our beef. We wanted to live off the land.

Bob: Were you planning on going to work when you moved?

Joe: She wasn't, but I was. I had been a welder and when we came back to look for a farm I found that I could get a job here as a welder. We thought about doing it without working out but I didn't think we would be able to do it. So we planned on my going to work.

The geographical move from a city to a small farm is far reaching. But the social and psychological change in moving from a home in the suburbs and a well-structured job in a bureaucracy to a rural area where an individual is a stranger to everyone he meets and most of the things he does, is undoubtedly much greater. So just as people contemplated where they might move and how they might secure a living, they also began to examine themselves to determine what old thoughts and habits they could transform into new potential. This personal change began where the desire to change one's residence had started--with the desire to simplify a lifestyle. But instead of contemplating a change of surroundings, many people paused to look inward. It was the difference between viewing life with a pair of binoculars and a microscope. If people were to change their lifestyles, they needed first to discover what they might do to foster that change. Developing potential within was so difficult that most were seldom aware when it began.

Sometimes they did not even know what was happening within and could only reconstruct their emerging feelings at a later time. They did know that coupled with the doubts, discontents, and desires to move, were longings to be quiet and serene. Some realized that changes had drifted in from the unconscious parts of their minds where culture unconsciously rubs and grates against itself to give uniqueness to each person. But now, as their thoughts turned inward, they focused on their desires to be more loving, giving, and caring. Initially these first images were faint, but became powerful and later played a significant role in helping people propel themselves into the future.

Perhaps the first insight some had that this change was occurring came with the realization that there was indecisiveness in their lives. When they began to think about another place to live, feelings of uncertainty surfaced. They did not know if such moves would allow them to be active participants in finding more meaning, or if moving would simply transfer or perhaps even add additional stress, tension, and anxiety to their lives. The indecision prompted almost everyone to examine the expressive parts of their lives and to undertake personal explorations.

Many found they were searching in a part of themselves they had not recently explored. They called it by a variety of names: a psychological, emotional, expressive, or even a spiritual part of themselves. Regardless of the name, they felt that they could develop a way to cope with the stress, anxiety, and frustration they had been experiencing. They felt that this discontent had arisen because they had misplaced their values and had put too much emphasis on success in material terms and too little on interpersonal relations. If they were to be better sustained, they felt they needed to make significant personal changes.

Many explored themselves through a craft or hobby, for almost everyone enjoyed such a pastime. When they were working with a craft or hobby, they could create what they wanted, move at their own pace, request help from others as needed, or experiment alone. Avocations provided an unobtrusive way to withdraw from the daily rush and search for new avenues of expression. It was possible to explore in new directions and create tangible expressions of thought.

The future migrants developed their skills in pottery, woodworking, ceramics, leathercrafts, carving, macrame, painting, or gardening. They spent hours fashioning objects. They became excited, enthused, and absorbed in what they were doing. Yet, their joy in learning new skills was tempered by the unexpected difficulty of mastering them. The effort took more time, effort, and self-discipline than they had imagined. The skills required more judgement, delicate moves, and a lighter touch than they had expected. But through their efforts, they were succeeding at doing something they had never attempted before.

Without exception, all were amazed at their own accomplishments. Their lives had new success stories. They learned they could develop new abilities. They had translated a thought, an idea, or a mood into a tangible bit of culture. Since they could create tangible objects, they reasoned, they could look deeper into themselves and discover the help and support which they needed to create new lifestyles.

This blacksmith talked about the creative process and changing lifestyles. We were riding in an old pick-up truck when he made these comments.

Darrel: The reason, Bob, why people have a great need to make something when they are transforming their lifestyles is because they need to authenticate themselves. Their daily lives have little meaning to them.

> Often their friends fail to interact with them. They need to know and learn about themselves. It's a crucial time. Do they still have value when so often no one tells them that they do? So they authenticate themselves. They create something which, really, is a part of themselves because they did it themselves. It reminds people that they are still unique and can make something of beauty or value.

Time spent in these creative activities was time spent in self-enriching discovery. Almost everyone found that they embodied a greater reservoir of emotions than they had previously thought. They found it possible to develop greater depth to the emotional side of their lives. They could be more sensitive, loving, joyous, happy, and giving than they had thought possible. But with the discovery of this greater depth came some unpleasant knowledge. Most also found that they had unknowingly allowed themselves to become rigid, demanding, and repetitious. Their inner lives had become stunted. They did not have sufficient emotional strength--nor the basic values, ethics, and beliefs which emotion mirrors--to sustain themselves adequately.

This was particularly true of those whose lifestyles had collapsed. These were the people who needed the greatest amount of internal strength, and yet they were so often the ones who had the least. The malady that afflicted them had too often robbed them of emotional strength, too. Those who had suffered a psychological collapse faced the greatest amount of internal rebuilding.

Often these people had to learn the importance of emotions to their lives. Many had been taught to believe that emotional expressions were signs of weakness and that they should be strong and endure against the so-called instability of sentiments, moods, and emotions. But they found feelings of anger and anxiety were coupled to a wider range of emotions and expressions than they had ever before known. They discovered they could locate and describe feelings which they had never before noticed.

At first these emotions were often expressed in unexpected ways. Some found, for instance, that it was difficult to make appropriate responses to activities which were going on around them. They laughed or were cynical when they should have cried, were nervous when others were relaxed, and became angry over minor irritations. They coveted privacy yet wanted to be public figures.

At times emotions emerged in waves. Opposite thoughts, moods, and feelings became interlocked. Anxiety and tension were tied to tenderness and caring. It was like having mental restraints on oneself. Those who were so affected had to take the time to break apart, analyze, and nurture these new and independent emotions. They had to learn to express their feelings of anger, hostility, fear, or love, tenderness, and caring, and to learn when such expressions were acceptable to others. And there were periods when mental stress caused emotions to cease. At times people could not state preferences--what they liked or disliked, how they felt, or what they wanted to do. During these times they found nothing within themselves. And then, at other times, moods varied greatly. Good times were quickly followed by bad times; creativity, action, and high energy were followed by periods of lethargy, inaction, and drowsiness--each mood cresting in rapid succession. And, in a great paradox, tensions and anxieties were intensified when the mind experienced periods of tranquility and joy. Sometimes the good times produced anxiety.

On a few occasions people discovered emotions which they could not tie to any particular experience in their past or visions of their futures. These feelings were extraneous and difficult to describe or explain but just seemed to dangle within and inevitably interrupt daily routines. They penetrated consciousness as fleeting thoughts, unusual daydreams, or nebulous preoccupations. It was as if a part of the mind had gone awry and acted independent of the wishes, desires, and actions of the person in whom it resided. And yet, even then, people found their minds were attempting to rectify this imbalance which existed. The mind seemed to be responsible for shedding its own insufficiency as it reached for growth and unity. People discovered that design and strength began to appear at the center of their minds. A foundation for the future was being built. This ceaseless desire of the mind to become a unity with the body became a powerful and ceaseless recurring theme.

And for still others an additional concern emerged. People discovered the debilitating effects of guilt in their lives. The guilt pushed them to do more and more, and reminded people that they had never before reached their potential. It was a permeating guilt which crested across their lives; one which they were only discovering.

Yet, perhaps more than anything, it was the recognition of this guilt which began to strengthen their lives. Through guilt they discovered what they had earlier suspected; they had expectations about living which they could not possibly meet and goals for their lifetimes which they could not accomplish. They could not work hard or fast enough to do everything they wanted and still have time to reflect on and enjoy their accomplishments. They expected too much both from themselves and others. Perfection was one of the attributes which they wanted, and anything short of it--from either themselves or others--was a sign of failure. They had left no room in their lives for celebration.

Here are the comments of yet another woman. This wife and mother of five children had left a career when she moved.

Marilyn: I felt guilty about myself. For years I had not been happy. I was working at what others wanted me to do. I didn't realize it at first but I was living my life through those people around me that I loved. I was inseparable and indistinguishable from them. I began to feel guilty because I wasn't me. When I realized that, I began to search for another way to live.

Perhaps the arts and crafts were more important to these people than to others. They needed tangible expressions of their thoughts, moods, and accomplishments. They talked with special pride about the awe-inspiring moments when they discovered they could create a vase from a lump of clay, a cabin from a pile of boards, or pick edible produce from the garden they had planted. They were developing direct and immediate expressions of their moods and feelings. They were succeeding, if only in a miniscule way, in breaking with everyday activities. They had successfully given direction to their lives. Fragile as these new abilities were, they were concrete indications that people could plan and successfully complete new tasks they had planned for themselves.

But slowly, even for those who felt great anguish, people began discovering some very nice things about themselves--things they had never before realized. They discovered that contrary to what they had believed, their efforts at work, in community affairs, and with their families had produced accomplishments. They had made contributions at work, and their families did respect their opinions. But these people had been too driven in the past to note their own achievements. In their haste to succeed, they had not even been aware of their own successes. Some people even discovered for the first time that they were intelligent and insightful. They had been so intent on meeting the demands of others that they did not know that they had abilities to work with extremely diverse groups, ideas, and situations. Yet their accomplishments had required that they contribute skills and abilities in difficult situations--and they had done so successfully. They simply had not been aware of their own skills and contributions.

This woman held several responsible and lucrative positions during her career. She was raising her own children and taking care of other relatives as well. Still, she had made and saved money. Her accomplishments were considerable. Yet, she had found it hard to believe that she was a competent person.

Anita: I started working as a file clerk. I liked my job and stayed with the company for many years. I went to school and worked hard. I volunteered for new tasks and soon I had several people working for me. Finally a whole department was under me and the major executives were still asking my opinion on other things. When the bosses were in town they used to come into my office and we would just sit there and talk and talk. But still I didn't think I could do anything. My family rarely encouraged me, yet they took my money. I was confused. I went to a psychologist and spent a lot of money with him. He gave me some tests and I learned I could do almost anything I wanted to do. I learned I had made money because I was competent and could get along with almost anyone. It was an amazing discovery for me.

Some people were surprised, too, when they discovered that they were sensitive. These were people who, in the past, had believed that they had not been responsive to others. And yet often, they were people who had participated in social concerns and issues and had made the hurts and struggles of others their own. They had responded to the needs of others--sometimes so quickly and intensely they had not cared for their own needs. Their responses had been so overwhelming that they had not even been aware of their own most sensitive feelings. They had been unable to detect where they had left off and others began.

Here is the story one personable forty year old man, a husband and father, told me. He remembered earlier times and pinpointed the period when his life turned around and he began the climb out of despair. He was the owner of his own shop at the time we talked.

Doug: All of a sudden the whole premise on which we based our concepts of how we lived and what we thought was right and wrong collapsed. Everybody was questioning everything--or at least I was. The people around me helped. They were inquisitive young people right out of college. Several of them were attorneys. They were still full of a whole lot of enthusiasm. I would tease them by saying, 'I wonder how long it's going to last before the corporate money gets you.' Instead of being disillusioned and remaining totally pessimistic, I achieved a degree of optimism. There was an alternative. There was... Listen! I've spent ever since then thinking about this. I stayed stoned for a whole year--it's true. I went through a tremendous amount of introspection and found myself wound up in knots. I didn't have any answers. But after that year, growth began because I began building. I began taking jobs. This is a guy who never learned how to change a light switch. Really! I never could build anything or do anything. I wasn't any good at it. I said, 'O.K., if you're turning around, why don't you turn around?' I did things like digging a two hundred fifty foot ditch through rock to put a guy's septic tank in. Why? I was broke. He said he was going to hire a backhoe to come in and do it and was bitching about the three hundred dollars he had to pay. I said, 'If it's all the same to you, you pay me and I'll do it.' It was an education. It was a big lesson in humility, too, I might add. Yes sir! I began to do odd jobs. I developed a great degree of enthusiasm--of self-confidence. I learned that I could do almost anything. It was invaluable. I had to learn all over that I had individuality and self-worth.

Bob: Where did you lose it? You had it once, didn't you?

Doug: No, I didn't. I never had a sense of individuality. Never!

Bob: How did you realize that you had never had it?

Doug: I realized that I had been much too willing to accept what others told me. Saneness and all that crap was a big trap. I don't care how many others bought it. Why did I? Why was I so willing not to question? When Vietnam came, why wasn't I out there protesting? I don't say that I should have been, but it never occurred to me to be a possibility. When I was younger, I never really knew I had a choice. I never questioned that I would go to college--my folks just sent me to college. I mean, what was I to do? To go to a vocational or technical school never crossed my mind. Anyway, I went to agriculture school which I think was a rebellion because my father wanted me to be an engineer. It was almost like trying to learn, at 30, to be an individual initially--not all over again.

Bob: It's better to do it then than at 40, isn't it?

Doug: Yes, but 40 isn't a lost cause either. I see lots of people who are beginning to become aware--50, 60, even 70 year old people. They say, 'Hey, wait a minute!!! There's something wrong!' I received a lot of love from people I previously hadn't been able to accept it from--nor been able to give it to. I have learned to say to a fellow man, 'I love you,' without feeling like he will accuse me of being a homosexual. I cannot be intimidated any more. I'm involved with human values that are worthwhile.

The inward search helped those who had collapsed to understand better their own abilities. They were finding that they were unique. They were discovering preferences in thoughts, moods, feelings, and values which had previously escaped them--and they were better able to state those preferences. Their struggles had been similar to others who had not experienced such total crises; only they were more personal, intense, and thorough.

Potential, fragile as it was, began to emerge. People had a glimpse of what they hoped their lives might become. And yet, the noticeable contrast still existed within. Trivia still ruled. Things they deemed important seldom found expression. Daily routines and activities were still largely meaningless. They found within themselves some love, joy, and happiness but with inadequate time to foster this new growth. They realized that they could preserve their present in their memories while moving into a new, more satisfactory future.

Those who had collapsed feared that they could not foster their new-found freedoms while remaining where they were. It was more than they could accomplish. They wanted to extricate themselves from their daily routines. To change, even if only into a situation which they knew little about, offered much more potential for growth. It would allow them, they believed, to express whatever was emerging within. Often these were the ones who put very little planning into their new effort. They attempted an abrupt break with their past.

But everyone who eventually moved apparently went through some introspection. None were immune from examining themselves. Almost without exception they began to believe they needed personal growth, and they believed the transition could make this possible. By looking inward they could simplify their lifestyles; the remaking of their worlds would follow. This insight helped restore order, balance, and clarity to their lives.

Several, while stating that change had often been a part of their lives, placed the anticipated move in a larger perspective. During their lifetimes their most firmly held beliefs regarding religion, life, death, family, and the nation had grown and matured--just as the body does. And as they reflected on the future, they felt it would be necessary again to go through change as they reached older age. So change, they reasoned, was as much a part of life as stability. This knowledge seemed to quiet some of their fears about moving.

Before moving, this husband and father had arrived at this conclusion:

> Bill: You know, you're always changing. From the time you're a baby until the day you die you're changing. We're here right now; when our child gets out of school, we may decide to go someplace else. I don't know. I do know you've got to keep changing all your life. You do change. You keep growing older. When we moved people asked us, 'How can you move and leave all your family and friends and everyone you've known all your life? You're leaving your home.' But that's not right. Home is wherever you are at any time. It's wherever you put down your roots. That's home.

And, almost everyone who moved raised some enduring questions that can never be resolved, or remain forever controversial. Could they live in an industrial society and remain the unique, kind, and caring individuals they wanted to be? Were they captives of the society around them and only reacting to what was happening? Or, was it possible to regain control of their lives in order to be the kind of people they wanted to be? Where were their abilities? Could they accomplish anything they wanted to? These were the existential questions which they discussed but could not resolve. But, the lack of an answer did not preclude them from moving.

The inward search to simplify a lifestyle that originally began as a vague etching on the mind developed into a demarcated roadmap of such a venture. Since people had examined themselves, they could make better decisions about the move. They began to understand their wants, directions, and the requirements of a successful move. By examination alone they gained additional knowledge of their abilities and increased their own competence. The sojourn into themselves was a fruitful part of the transition and began to change their lives.

This family took several years to discover the opportunities available to them. They reported having more fun making their decisions than anyone else I encountered. Earlier in the conversation they had told of extreme frustration with the city in which they lived. But by talking and trying new experiences, this couple became aware of their potential before they moved.

Joan: When I quit my job, things just opened up. Life got simpler, immediately! I felt bad about leaving and I missed the people some, but not for very long. I started going around with my husband. He was making things in his shop out of wood, cabinets, shelves, toys and things like that. I would help him and then we had to take them out and sell them. It was so much fun. We were so free. I began talking to people about woodworking. We bought and sold antiques. I had a big garden which I loved. Life took on such a different meaning. I gained a lot of confidence.

Bill: Yes, I quit my job years before she did. And we always vacationed a lot together. We'd go to the mountains skiing or to the seashore. Just before we came here we went scuba diving in Jamaica for two weeks.

Joan: So we always had lots of fun. That was new to me. He taught me how to do what I liked to do--to have fun.

Bob: Why didn't you stay there and change your lifestyle? Why did you have to move?

Bill: Well, like I told you, our neighbors didn't understand us. They liked us but they thought we were crazy. They would get up and go to work each morning. But we didn't. We'd just go to our shop behind the house. They spent money for gas and lunch; we didn't. She had a garden and we lived from that. I made all the repairs on the cars and around the house. There wasn't much expense there. And we made money buying, selling, and trading. And I had all this equity in the house. But the neighbors were really getting cold to us. This one I told you about drove an hour each way to work and then worked another job, too. He didn't understand. But he didn't have to do that. He could have changed. And the taxes and restrictions of the city got to be too much. We had to change.

Joan: So we made a big mistake. (They both laughed loudly at this statement.) We sold the house and got a lot of money from it and bought a motor home. We toured the United States for a whole year. Twice we went across it and back. We had fun. It was expensive but we had fun. And we blew much of the money we got from the house. The reason we're successful now is because we spent three years talking about what we wanted and liked to do. We know ourselves.

People developed a new sense of purpose as they made their personal decisions about moving. For most the period was very exciting. Only a very few were able to make quick decisions. For most, the decisions took time. One family thought about the prospects for twenty years, another attempted to work out a change twice before actually moving on the third attempt. Most people took years to finalize their plans. No one wanted to fail.

They did not want to move and then discover they lacked skills, money, or strength for such a transition. They would have found it overly embarrassing to return to their old neighborhoods and admit to families and friends that the move had been unwise. Most were thorough in their considerations.

Many places were examined. Some even told of giving consideration to Australia or South America. But foreign countries were distant and difficult to reach and were quickly rejected. Most people believed staying in the United States was a much more logical alternative. Usually, they quickly decided on a rural area and looked at those areas which were already experiencing an influx of residents--the Northeast, Southwest, Northwest, Alaska, and the Ozarks. They talked to friends who had visited the areas, studied maps, wrote to realtors, and planned vacations where they might eventually want to move. They wanted to know which areas held the most advantages and the fewest drawbacks.

Those who eventually chose the Ozarks believed that the area embodied the attributes which attracted them to rural life. The climate encompassed neither the tremendous heat of the South nor the frigid cold of the North. Land was relatively cheap. Agriculture was an established way of life. And, perhaps above all, independent action and interpersonal cooperation already existed. Many believed it an ideal place to live.

Generally husbands first encouraged the moves. They seemed to encounter more stress at work and with family and community commitments. Often they were the first who professed the need to live differently and indicated the willingness to find a new place to live and develop new skills. But sometimes wives encouraged the moves. They felt stress in their own lives, remembered the scenery and beauty of the Ozarks from past trips, and believed that change would be a developmental experience. But if they, too, had careers then even more discussion and planning for the move was necessary. This joint planning strengthened the prospects for a move and enriched the relationship of the two. On a few occasions, couples simultaneously left careers behind.

This is what a housewife and mother of three elementary-aged boys told me about their family's decision to move.

Sue: It is something you have to be psychologically ready for, otherwise I don't think it would ever work. And I wasn't ready years ago when my husband was ready to leave. My sister did a similar thing four years ago. She had never been out of Boston. She packed up with her family and went to Utah. She said she would never go back. So we finally got out to see her. That sort of clinched our decision. We saw how happy she was to get away from the rat-race and the traffic and everything else.

At other times both spouses simultaneously reached the decision to move.

Elaine: I think it was pretty well fifty-fifty. We talked for two years about what it would be like someplace else before we actually left. We did quite a bit of research on where to move. Then we decided to go.

Families with children were concerned about how their children would be affected. The ages of the children had a strong influence on attitudes toward the move. Younger children in grade school usually made the change with anticipation and enjoyment. But older children, those in their teens, often balked at the prospects. They had friendships and school routines which they did not want to disrupt. It appeared that families with older children made fewer moves.

Families were concerned about what their children would learn. They wanted a place where their children would be free to roam in the countryside, hunt, fish, play in the woods, and make a garden. They believed that the outdoors and a small farm were preferable to urban life. But they also wanted a good education for their children. Most were conscious of the advantages of a formal education and did not want to take this possible alternative away from their children. Some began by considering educating their children at home. They wondered if they could develop their own curriculum, or find a suitable course of instruction which would allow them to be the teachers of their own children. Many, though, felt this would be a herculean task and settled on finding a good rural school system. They were somewhat apprehensive about finding elementary, junior, and senior high schools which would prepare their children for good colleges and universities.

But schools were only one of the community services people wanted. They were aware that even though they wanted to simplify their lifestyles, there were other services which they would need. After all, in the urban areas they had become accustomed to shopping centers, movies, grocery stores, and dry cleaners. They knew they would need some of them after the move. So, they considered the availability of these facilities.

As people contemplated the complex decisions, they noticed that major changes were taking place within them. They had begun thinking about a move as a way to escape the ills of urban life. But the more they thought about the possibilities, the more they viewed the moves as enriching and growth-giving experiences, not merely as escape. They became less bound by traditions and routines and more absorbed in what the future had to offer. The future, not the past, began to guide their lives. Their search for potential had come full circle.

CHAPTER IV

OFF TO THE COUNTRY

Eventually, a time came when a decision had to be made. People could study, plan, make trips to the Ozarks, search themselves, and dream about what could be. But if they were to move, they had to complete plans, decide to move, sell the old house, purchase property, and arrange for the move. These were always intense and exciting times.

The final decisions were made in different ways. Every story was unique. Few of the final decisions, however, were made during times of philosophical thought or introspection. Rather, people encountered a nuisance which frustrated and upset them. Often, this nuisance was a repetitive event which they had earlier chosen to ignore, deemed inconsequential, or had viewed as a part of life which needed to be endured. Often the episode was "the straw that broke the camel's back." These common occurrences--such as getting caught in another traffic jam, having another run-in with the boss, watching someone else on the job being rewarded for unproductive labor, or returning home from a vacation to a pile of paper work at the office--were viewed as infringements on their own lives. Often people were mad when they decided to move. They had been fouled one too many times.

This interview was held in a small store several miles from the nearest town. Customers, delivery men, and the merely curious listened to our conversation and then interrupted when they grew weary and needed service. This family made their final decisions very quickly.

Sarah: We had been on vacation to California and on the way home John said, 'I've got to get out of this rat race.' You know how you feel when your vacation is over and you've got to get back to work. He said, 'I have got to get out of the rat race.' Previous to this a couple of the men, slightly older than he, had suffered heart attacks. One had died on his way home from vacation from a heart attack. He went just like that. He said, 'I've got to get out of the rat race.' When we got home... you know that stack of literature that comes in the mail and is waiting for you after a two week vacation.... right on top was a real estate circular advertising this place.

Bob: And it was there just by luck?

John: Who knows?

Bob: God put it there?

Sarah: I guess. You never know about these things. But at any rate, he said, 'Well, let's go down and look at it.' For many many years he had wanted a business of his own. And we looked. We had been on the verge before. In two instances we actually bought into businesses. Then the company made him such an offer he couldn't refuse. Then we got out of the business--either sold it to somebody or just backed out. So I thought, 'Oh, a weekend in the Ozarks. It might be pretty.' I expected nothing to come of it. And when he saw the place I tried to get him to stay for a weekend and look at it. But we had a dinner date with friends on Saturday night. We came down Thursday night, saw the place on Friday, and left Saturday morning.

Bob: Did you know much about the Ozarks?

John: We knew nothing. We had never been down here before.

Bob: This was your first trip to the Ozarks?

Sarah: The only trip to the Ozarks. We flew into Springfield and drove no farther than this. We never looked over the surrounding area. There could have been a supermarket around the bend in the road and we wouldn't have known it. We used no common sense whatsoever.

Bob: This is the only place you came to?

Sarah: The only place. We looked at nothing else. We have no right to be a success. I mean, actually, it should have failed dismally! But we were here for two or three hours, made them an offer, and went back to the hotel in Springfield. The real estate agent called up and said they accepted the offer. He came down with the papers and we left the next morning.

Bob: And you owned it!

John: And we owned it. Within a month we were down here for good. So as I say, I'm still scratching my head over that one. From then on we took all the gamble out of it.

Perhaps this family was able to make this quick decision because they had planned previous moves which had not worked out. Those attempts may have given them a base from which to make such a decision. They had thought, worried, read, been concerned, traveled, and discussed enough to know that an alternative was sensible--at least for them. For most, though, the final decision was made in a much more deliberate way. Families studied the move, thought about what they wanted, considered what might be done, and made trips to the Ozarks to see what they could learn.

This couple told me about their discontent with urban life and what they had hoped to accomplished by moving to the Ozarks. Their preparation for making the decision was more thorough than most, and they were pleased with the effort that went into planning their move:

Judy: I think one of the reasons why we decided to make the move was because we had a subscription to the *Mother Earth News.* We read an awful lot about the good life, survival on fives acres, and things of that nature.

Chris: A lot of people are full of starry-eyed ideas when they make a move to the farm. They are quite surprised when they do get there. We were fortunate that we looked around a bit before we decided on this piece of property. We began looking in Arkansas first. We found that the way a piece of property is described in a magazine is a lot different than what it really is. 'Gently rolling countrysides' become deep hills. As a matter of fact, you have to have cows with two short legs to walk up and down them. Cute cottages become cabins where the retreat facilities are outside and there are no bath facilities whatsoever--except a quarter of a mile down the road at a creek where the waterfall is. We understood this before we put our money down. But I know people who bought property over the telephone and were very surprised when they came down to see it.

Bob: Did you make a lot of plans before you actually moved?

Judy: Oh Yes! We talked about it for a year and a half to two years.

Chris: Yes! Looking into it! Trying to understand the move. From the income to the cultural shock--the difference in lifestyle--trying to anticipate what to expect so that we could understand the differences that we ran into so it wouldn't come as a shock.

Bob: When you considered moving you looked in Arkansas and then you said you purchased this place. Were you satisfied when you found this?

Judy: That is a difficult question. We were pleased. After we looked in Arkansas at a cabin with the outside plumbing I made the comment to Chris that I had changed my mind. I wanted a bathroom and a hot bath. Those were two things that I was going to insist on. Until that time I didn't put any stipulations on size of property or house or anything. But after we saw the cabin with a waterfall for a shower we decided that we would have indoor plumbing. So that changed our whole point of view.

Bob: You had been considering anything until then?

Judy: Just anything. There were no limits. We just didn't set any restrictions when we came down. We thought we'd see what was available. We thought we'd develop our parameters as we went along; then bring everything into our financial capability. There was one thing we did not understand. When you look at a house for sale in the Chicago area, they don't mention indoor or outdoor plumbing. So, really, when we came down to look at property, it didn't dawn on us that they didn't have indoor plumbing.

Chris: She was quite distressed about that!

Judy: I didn't like the idea of walking one-fourth mile to the waterfall in order to take a shower.

Chris: You didn't tell him the whole story. When we looked at the place a girl was walking up the road and she was sweating like a pig. The realtor asked her what she had been doing. She said she had been taking a bath. He asked her where she took a bath. She said, 'One-fourth a mile down the road by the creek there is a little waterfall and that is where I take my bath.' And here she was walking back up. I said to myself, 'if I have to sweat that much getting back it doesn't make much sense going down there to get in the water.' We decided then to look at the picture a little differently. A place without electricity would have been difficult. We grew up with television and I felt that we would probably want to continue watching it. We decided that there would have to be indoor plumbing and electricity. We had no set idea as to the size of the house, property, or anything. We came across this quite by accident. We had gone to a sportsman's show in Chicago and picked up a little magazine called "The Ozarks Playground." There was a little paragraph in there from a local businessman and all it said was, 'You'll like our little town. Write to me and I'll tell you all about it.' So I wrote to him. He wrote back and said, 'Come on down. We'll show you around.' We came down and they treated us real nice. They took us out to lunch and everything. They introduced us to a real estate agent. We started looking. We came across this place which was quite run down because it hadn't been farmed for over ten years. The weeds were so high I wasn't even aware that there was a barn out there. It was just covered with weeds. The fences were down and all kinds of stuff like that.

Judy: But we liked the location because it was on a blacktopped road and was close enough to town--and yet not in town. I learned a long time ago about zoning restrictions and how much better it would be on a farm outside the city limits. Now I think the city is slowly coming this way and may encroach on us one of these days. I hope not. At the time we bought the place the real estate agent said he hoped it wouldn't be too lonely out here for us. It actually suited me just fine; but since then they have been building and there has been more traffic on this road than ever before. I think it is too crowded now--much too crowded.

Chris: So we ended up here. It was only afterwards that we found out--to our good fortune--that we have a sound several hundred foot well with spring water that is absolutely soft. That's something you don't usually find on a farm. We're on the main feeder line for the electricity to the next town. If our electricity is out it's out in town, too. So, they fix it in a hurry. We don't have three days delay in getting it fixed. It's easy to get to our place.

Another alternative, which a few chose, was to sell their property in the urban area, get their money, and move before looking for land. Usually those who did this planned on living in more than one place after the move and taking even a year or two to find a permanent home.

This man and his wife told me about their decision to leave as we sat around their kitchen table one Saturday morning. He had pressures at work and disliked driving in heavy traffic. Both were disturbed that city ordinances required them to make renovations to their urban home.

David: I had thirty-five men working for me when I left. But there were customers on one side of me, the union on the other, and the company on top of that. One day the boss made me mad again and I told him as soon as I could sell my house I would be gone. Luckily, the first guy that looked at the house liked it. He made me an offer and he owned it in ten days. We didn't know where we were going for sure.

Bob: Marcie, What did you think about the move?

Marcie: We talked about it. Both of us decided that it was time to leave. He was young enough to do what he wanted and our three children were in elementary school so a move wouldn't ruin their lives.

Bob: But you did talk about it?

Marcie: Oh yes. In fact, we subscribed to the Springfield newspaper for about a year before we made our move. We had traveled through here going to St. Louis on a vacation. He liked the out-of-doors and fishing. We tried to pick this general area. We never did decide on a town before the move.

Bob: When did you move?

David: In March. When we left it was a nice, sunshiny, warm day. There was snow on the ground when we arrived here.

Marcie: We rented a truck. My dad brought his truck. Joe drove the rental truck and I drove the station wagon. My grandmother lived with us at the time, so the kids, me, and my grandmother came in the car.

Bob: You moved where?

Marcie: Marshfield, first. My mother was living there at the time. She supposedly had a big farmhouse rented there and we were going to stay with her for a while. But when we got there it had been sold out from under her. So we had about a month to decide where we were going to live. It was complicated finding another place so quickly, but in a month we had purchased trailers to live in. We moved to another nearby town.

David: We wanted to rent, but I think that there just wasn't anything available that we wanted to live on.

Marcie: We wanted a farm. We stayed in the trailer park about a year. In the meantime we bought this farm, but it didn't have a house on it. We moved the trailer out here. But before we ever got the trailer set up a tornado came through and turned it upside down. We never got to live in it before the tornado. It did substantial damage and we didn't have any insurance. But we rebuilt it and moved into it and lived in it for several years. Then, we built this house.

Locating and deciding on the piece of property which was to become a new home was seldom simple. Several began looking for property months and even years before moving to the Ozarks. Most obtained area newspapers, catalogs from national farm realty companies, and popular "back-to-the-land" magazines. These sources helped provide information on various parts of the United States, comparative prices for land in each area, and the amount of money that would be needed for the initial purchase.

Even the normal procedure of finding a farm, selling a piece of property in the urban area, and then moving had disconcerting moments. Usually, property was found and purchased on a trip to the Ozarks before the actual move was made. Often it was the equity in the old home that became the down payment for the new property. This resulted in anxious moments as people manipulated two different transactions. Usually, people hoped to find an old, run-down farm house on a few acres. The price, they reasoned, would be less if they could do some of their own repairs. But, this was the dream of many, and so very few found such homes. Most purchased small existing structures or mobile homes.

> *Here's the story of one young family's excursion into the Ozarks to purchase property. Many people found they had to be persistent when dealing with realtors. This family had only a long week-end to look before purchasing.*
>
> Leonard: Before we moved we wrote to an agency and were getting pamphlets in the mail every day about farms in this area. I spotted several that I liked in the realty catalog about this area. I called and talked to the realtor and told him I was coming out. I wanted to see him. We came back, but he went on vacation after we told him we were coming. I called his house and his daughter said, 'Well, Daddy's on vacation. You could talk to a friend of his who works nights.' I talked with him, but he didn't know anything about us. I got upset. As we started to leave town I stopped at another realty office just as they were closing for the day. They said they had several places they could show us and asked us to come back the next day. We got a hotel room and spent the night. When we came back the next morning, we told them how much we wanted to spend and what we were looking for. They had this place, which belonged to the owner's sister. She said we could go down and look at it if we wanted to. So we came down and it was in the right price range--which was the main reason we bought it. I didn't want to saddle myself with large payments. That's how we ended up finally getting this place. It was cheap.

Once the final decision to move had been made, neighbors, friends, and family had to be told. Telling others often produced surprises. Separation from loved ones is always difficult, but since such moves were largely voluntary, "good-bys" were complicated. The reactions of acquaintances varied. Family and friends could support a move for the sake of a promotion, transfer, or pay raise, but found a move for "less money"difficult to understand. Those who felt the move would bring their about-to-depart friends more "freedom," more time to themselves, and get them out of the industrial rat race encouraged the move. Others, who believed such a venture would rob families and children of money and opportunities, attempted to dissuade them. They pointed out the pit-falls of the anticipated move. Or, as another reaction, associates often confided about themselves. Those who were unhappy wished they had the courage to make a similar move. Some told of contemplating such a move earlier in life but felt they now had too much invested to consider such a move--at least not until they retired. And, a few friends felt the move was a repudiation of them and their way of life. They became angry at those who would soon depart. But inevitably family and friends wanted to be kept informed of the move. They wanted to know if it was possible to move to the country and simplify a lifestyle.

This executive decided to give up a large income when he moved with his family to the Ozarks. Some of his friends were astounded.

Bob: What did people where you worked say when you told them you were going to move to a small farm?

Mark: Well, I had quite a few friends at the office. They just could not believe that a member of the board of directors would just up and leave the company. It had never happened before in the company's history. It's not a very big company. But, they just couldn't believe that I was going to leave and, of all things, go to a farm and work at small-town wages. They were horrified that I would work for minimum wages.

Nancy: That was the hardest thing for people to accept. Somebody giving up money to go do something for less.

Bob: Did you find people saying to you, 'Hey, I wish I had done what you are doing?'

Mark: Oh, yes. One of them said he would love to do something like this, but he didn't want to give up what he had.

Here's the way another family went about telling their family, neighbors, and friends about their decision.

Bob: How did you tell people?

Mary: Well, we just told them. We said, 'Hey, we're going to do this.' We really had not talked too much to people outside of our family about ever doing this. Everyone was pretty shocked that we had ever even considered it. Most businessmen that Jim told, because he had to tell them he was leaving, envied and admired him for trying. Several made comments like, 'I wish I had tried that kind of thing years ago, but now I can't.' For a lot of people, though, it was 'Well, it's not for me but I admire you for trying.' But people were very interested in knowing how things went. They wanted us to correspond and let them know how things were going.

Bob: What were the reactions of your families?

Mary: My family thought we were nuts for even thinking about it. They still think we're crazy. Jim's family was very supportive. Of course, they came from a more rural background.

The actual move--the process of gathering one's belongings and literally making the trek--was a symbol of the past and future coming together in the present. The past was evident when all the experiences of those who moved was brought to bear on a single act. The future manifested itself in hopes and dreams. For eventually, it happened. The old house was sold--the new one purchased. Employment ceased. Normally, every family member took part in packing boxes. And since corporate ties had been broken, the family usually secured a rental truck to save as much money as possible. One member would drive the rental truck while the others followed in the family vehicle. The plans for a new way of life were becoming an integral part of the present. For many the journey was their Rubicon.

Here is the usual process as told by a mother who engineered a move from the West Coast.

Debbie: Yes, and everything went perfect. We rented a big truck that was packed to the gills. Behind that we towed our pickup truck which was packed and we looked like the Beverly Hillbillies. I was behind my husband in the station wagon. All of our friends were crying and

> praying when we pulled out of the driveway. They didn't think we would get out of town. And we made it here without a lick of trouble. Like I say, I think the move was really meant to be. We are very happy.

Those who moved were thrown, sometimes for the first time, on their own resources. The future they strove for was still ambiguous while the past contributed very little to their present. No amount of preparation could have been totally sufficient, for they would need judgement, strength, and resources as yet untested. Still, they had intentionally made the decision to change their lifestyles. Most were very optimistic about their futures.

CHAPTER V

THE CHALLENGE

Once people moved, hopes and dreams were their primary resources for the future. Daily routines, left behind but days before, might as well have been ancient history, for previous experiences were no longer useful guides for their actions. Life was exciting, for every action set precedents for the future.

The first days and even weeks passed in a flurry of activities. The new house had to be cleaned, the trailer unloaded, and boxes unpacked. Decisions had to be made about where the family's belongings would be kept. Utilities needed to be turned on, the first major shopping trips made, and in the midst of this, the family had to eat, sleep, and find time to encourage one another. These were hectic times.

The newness of the situation added zest to the experience. The house, no matter how well it was inspected before being bought, still contained surprises: another closet, a larger wall, or a new view of the out-of-doors. And outside, particularly if the family lived on a farm for the first time, myriads of new adventures were discovered. Family members became involved in observing wildlife, from bugs and beetles to squirrels, snakes, and soaring hawks. They planned the garden, explored barns, and took time to watch the setting sun. It was as if people could "absorb" the pleasure of the new adventures.

Because there were so many new activities, families often focused their near-total attention on accomplishing the tasks which needed to be done. The new residents experienced a burst of energy. They barely noticed that establishing a new home was even more time consuming and difficult than they had anticipated. But, because they were working so hard and enjoying what they were doing, they were succeeding at moving to the country.

When people reflected on this first frenzied activity, it was not uncommon for them to state that they had been motivated because of the size of the task. They discovered that they were people who enjoyed a challenge; and part of their motivation was due to the pleasure they derived from mastering a difficult task.

This young couple regarded the move as a challenge.

Lana: I think when we came here it was a challenge. Remember, we had on our minds that if we fell on our faces we were still young enough to go back to Baltimore.

Jerrry: Well, not Baltimore. We would go someplace else.

Lana: But, we were still young enough to do it. We looked at it as a challenge. Can we do it on our own without a company that pays for time off and paid vacations? Can I work on a farm as hard as anyone?

Bob: But at some point you obviously felt you had conquered the challenge?

Jerry: I think so. We proved it by moving here in the first place under adverse conditions--which is a physical shock--by selling our house, putting everything in little cardboard boxes, and moving here where we don't have a genealogy. We don't have a mother or a father or an aunt or an uncle that we can call when we have a problem. They are 1,000 miles away.

Almost everyone expressed happiness and excitement, particularly with all the new farming activities they attempted. Once in a while they over-extended their abilities in their zeal to try a new venture.

It was common for families, as with this one with three small children, to attempt many new endeavors. This family was here only a few months when we discussed their first impressions of the Ozarks.

Bob: Do you feel like you just dropped in and tasted a little bit of everything?

Sue: Yes, most people go through ten years to get what we have come through already. The first day we moved in we went right out and got the kids two white rabbits. The woman we bought the rabbits from let us pick them out of the cage. I said, 'Well, we want two of the same sex.' She said, 'Well, you really can't tell at this age.' So I said, 'Oh, O.K.' So we brought the rabbits home. I knew rabbits reproduced but I didn't know how fast. The kids loved their little rabbits. They got up and fed them and everything. The second day after we moved in, my husband brought home two heifers that were eight months old at the time. I was expecting little calves but he comes in with two great big heifers. So that was the second day. Then he decided he wanted chickens. That was in May. Now we've got laying hens that we get eggs from--ten laying hens and twenty-five butchering chickens. So we got through that. It was about that time that we realized that we had a male and a female rabbit. So the one got pregnant. She had a litter of six. They got to be pretty good sized, and our cat got in and killed three of them. So we had to bury them. Then, a month later she had another litter of five. That's when we sold the rabbits. Forget the rabbits.

We used to let the rabbits run all around the barn lot. We never kept them in a cage. They would go into the barn to their cage only at night. They were pets. Then we got the pigs. We jumped into that. We raised them. One had arthritis. Every day for a week I had to go out and give him a shot. Then one came down with pneumonia. So we've learned a bit about pigs. And our herd of cattle has been growing. We leased out our land when we first moved here. The man who had his cattle on our land had one cow that dropped a calf on our property. She had so much milk she had to be milked out, or partially milked out, by hand. I knew a little bit about milking a cow so I used to help. I would milk her for him so he wouldn't have to come by. Then another cow of his dropped a calf on our property. It was a month old and died. Mike wasn't home at the time and the kids and I stood out there and watched the calf die. We figured it must have choked to death. I didn't know what to do for it. I called the owner. By the time he got here the calf was just about dead. So that was our first real heartbreak. It took me days to get over that because it was really a cute calf. I had fallen in love with it.

For most, no task was any more important than finding employment. Only a very few had enough resources to go without jobs, or could make sufficient incomes from farming. Some were able to put employment off for a while and others worked at several different or part-time jobs. But eventually, almost every family had to have at least one wage earner. Like most other things, finding suitable employment was challenging. Jobs were not plentiful. The pay in the Ozarks was invariably less than other places. Normally, people could find only seasonal work in the tourist industry, commute many miles daily to better paying permanent jobs in the larger towns, or start their own businesses. Those few who became craftsmen had to find markets for their work. Often, the need for income made it necessary for both husband and wife to work.

This husband and father was skilled as an auto mechanic. He took some time to discover the most satisfactory way to pursue his trade.

Ed: When we first moved here, we had already sold our home, and so we had a few dollars saved. We took a month to travel the entire area. Every day we traveled around talking to people. I visited with a lot of other mechanics who had shops. One man told me he would hire me when the tourist season began. But that was several months away. Several others wouldn't talk to me at all because I was new in the area. But finally, one man began talking to me. I hung around his shop for three days and we talked. Finally, he told me to move my tools in and go to work. I thought that was a good place. He had been here all of his life. He knew everybody. I convinced him that I was a good mechanic.

For some, the challenges were greater than for others. Either people did not have the necessary skills to accomplish what they set out to do, or they undertook something unique, or the task was just an extremely large one. Often these were things that people "had just wanted to do."

This newly married couple attempted only one new experience--building their own house. It was truly a fine structure built mostly from native materials. But it was a burdensome challenge since they hardly knew how to use a hammer before they began. Yet, their attempt was successful. They overcame every difficult obstacle. It was a herculean task. We sat in their new living room, and much of the evening was spent listening to their description of the house, how they decided to build it, and what its completion meant to them.

Bob: Jan, I like your house.

Jan: Well, we decided we wanted to build a house using native materials as much as possible. We wanted to build as cheaply but as substantial as possible. Those were the requirements. We also built it on a hill. We spent about a year and a half getting it to this point. It was quite a year and a half.

Bob: Why don't you describe your house?

Jan: Well, it's about 20 x 30 in this room. It is 60 feet across the back of the house. We've also got a bedroom back there. The house has a vaulted ceiling. There's a bedroom, studio, and darkroom upstairs to meet our art needs. We have a nice view of the big rolling hills out of the front window. We watch the sun set over there every evening. This is a glade area.

James: Right. We found a site that we liked. We bought the land with a partner. We bought 109 acres. It is a long, narrow piece of land. I wanted the view, which we got. It was a completely level place. We had to take out about four trees to build the house. It's setting on bed rock. We hit rock on the back side maybe 3 1/2 feet down and it runs out to solid rock on the front. We selected it primarily for the view. We just dropped 'er right in.

Jan: I know something else we have to tell you. It's how we got our house designed. We knew we were going to start building and we decided that we would figure out some ideas of our own. We started putting it together--dimensions and arranging rooms next to each other--and we came up with a house that we liked pretty well. Then we thought, well, let's just look a little bit more and make sure this is what we want. James got some vacation home plan books and we found a plan that was almost identical to what we had drawn up ourselves. We went ahead and sent off for the plans so that we would have something to start with when it came to actually laying out the foundation. Then we started changing everything again because building with oak is so much different than standard building techniques. We know where all the changes are on the originals. We've adapted it. For instance, the balcony would have been free standing but because of the weight of the roof we had to put these supports down to catch the weight of the roof. There are structural changes all the way through it.

Bob: Yet, it looks elegant!

James. It's crazy. I don't think anybody else would build a house like this. The wall studs are 2" x 6" green oak studs on 16" centers. As you can see we've got 4" x 4" and 4" x 6" supports on the roof. The rafters are laminated beams. Each is over thirty feet long. Green, they weigh 600 pounds apiece.

Bob: How did you get them up there?

James: We built them across the balcony and the back part of the house on top of the second story. Then we laid the beams down across the top.

Bob: How did you get them up on that balcony?

James: We built them up there in sections.

This couple went on for over another hour describing with great pride and in minute detail this house they had built. They described the structural design, the roof which was strong enough "to drive a tank over," the insulation, and the wood heating unit. But even after that, we continued on the subject for a while longer.

Bob: Well, you two really did a lot of work on this house!

Jan: Oh yes! Then I got pregnant with Jennifer and that kind of...

James: I don't know when you had time or I had the strength. But somehow you did it.

Jan: When they started working on the roof, I got pregnant. My doctor said no lifting and no climbing ladders, but I could do anything else. Well, that was right when we started putting shingles on the roof. That knocked me out of helping there.

James: You helped put the studs up. The stuff weighs six or eight pounds a board foot when green. We figured out one day how many tons of lumber we moved. We had a lumber truck deliver it. They hydraulically lifted the pile and drove out from under it. We ended up with this wood sitting like a straw pile. If the wood had dried like that it would have warped. We had to stack it flat. We ended up moving just an incredible amount. I think we figured six tons a day--just the two of us.

Jan: A board at a time.

James: We hired a guy who did the plumbing and electrical work. Actually until about half way through I didn't know what I was doing. But then I knew. I could see that everything was going to fit together.

Jan: We had the kind of plans which kept giving the details step by step, 'put this board first, that one next.'

James: Well, we kind of fumbled through it together.

Bob: Had you been a craftsman before? Did you view this as an effort to be a craftsman and work with your own hands?

James: In a way I did. I just wanted to get out of the city. I had no idea what was going on when I came down. We lived in a tent back of the kitchen. We had a two-man tent.

Bob: I hope this was the summertime.

Jan: Yes! We came down in August. It got into wintertime and it got cold and it rained every day. There was nothing but mud. And we had the dog. The lightning and the rain...

James: And working with the foundation. We had to suction all the water out of the foundation.

Jan: We had to put a hose in and suck it out. We dug the foundation by hand. We poured most of it after we got the water out. We made a four foot mistake on the foundation so we had to go back and dig that out by hand. We had to mix the cement in a wheel barrow. It was a hell of a lot of work.

James: Understatement!

Bob: Like crossing the Pacific in a rowboat?

Jan: Yes.

James: But I learned how to hammer.

Jan: Winter was coming on here!

James: So we went to our friends. They rescued us.

Jan: They have a bunk house. They took us in and we lived in one end of a 10 x 15 foot bunk house. We stayed there for the rest of the winter and then in the spring as soon as it was warm enough, we wanted to be on our own. The guys worked real hard to get the bedroom finished enough so that we could live in it. We moved into the bedroom. We had a Coleman stove and no water. Our well was not dug. We hauled water in but had no plumbing. I think our power was in but it was temporary so we didn't want to run too much at one time. It was a pretty good experience.

Of all the experiences in which people were involved during the first year, food production and preservation often had the greatest impact. They became major rallying points in the challenge which people encountered. The growing, caring for, harvesting, and preserving of food was something many wanted to do. They placed a special emphasis on growing their own food.

But it was a long way from being philosophical about raising food and actually going out and cultivating a large garden. Most families discovered immediately that gardening meant a lot of hard work. They had to learn what varieties to select and how much to plant, when to plant, the amount of fertilizer to use, what tilling needed to be done, the way insecticides could be used, when to harvest and how to preserve what was grown. If the garden was to be organically grown, another whole orientation to gardening had to be developed. There were decisions to be made about the cost and size of the garden. If some of the work was to be done with a large, or even small tractor, the new arrivals had to obtain that tractor. Normally, families found a neighbor to plow and disc the garden plot. Whenever they could, they read books, articles, and talked about gardening with their friends. They discovered that their efforts had a direct relationship to the quality of their gardens. Their daily efforts were crucial.

There were occurrences over which the family had little or no control. Rain, wind, insects, and disease all played a part in the garden productivity. It was the first time people had to depend directly on the natural elements for their supply of food. Gardening required them to have faith that the plants would bear. And yet, that faith was justified. Families discovered they could garden. Normally rain fell, seeds grew into plants, winds weren't too hot, and insects were controlled. Nearly every family became aware of the difference between working at a job, receiving a paycheck, and going to the store to buy highly processed food, and purchasing seed, tending a garden, and sitting down to a meal of food they had grown themselves. People discovered a new relationship between themselves and the soil. They gained a more direct appreciation of the earth and they found the work both humbling and exalting. They took a secret pride in growing gardens.

Here's a typical statement about what gardening meant. These people were already gardeners when they moved to the Ozarks. Others learned the skills after they arrived.

Jack: She had a very beautiful garden last year even when it was so dry. Her garden produced so much!

Beverly: I had to water it, but I didn't use any water from our well. I put out some large barrels and caught rain water in them and siphoned water from that into small buckets and carried it to the garden.

Bob: What did you grow in your garden?

Beverly: We have a beautiful asparagus patch. The people who lived here before us planted it and took good care of the ground it was on. So the asparagus grows well. I think people around here often only grow beans, potatoes, tomatoes, and corn. But I like to grow lots of different kinds of vegetables. Ever year I experiment with new vegetables or varieties. I raise peas, squash, beans, lettuce, cabbage, potatoes, several kinds of tomatoes, zucchini, and corn.

Bob: Do you both work in the garden?

Beverly: We compliment each other a lot. I like to work in the garden and actually grow things. I care for the plants, harvest the produce, and preserve it. But he's a more diligent weeder than I am. He weeds around the fence line and the outside of the garden. He's neater than I am. And, he helps me get our son to help in the garden when he doesn't want to. He's better at that than I am. So, I think we compliment each other.

Bob: Does most of your food come from the garden?

Beverly: The garden is a supplement to our food supply. We nibble off of it a lot in the summertime. We eat lots of salads, tomatoes, onions, and radishes straight from the garden. And I canned lots of things--tomatoes and home-made spaghetti sauce. And I freeze lots of things, too. And it saves us money, too. It lowers our grocery bill. It also provides recreation for us. We work in the garden instead of going places. We don't have to buy gasoline. That's good for us. And it turns our mind to recycling because we turn all of our refuse into organic matter for the garden. It reminds us that we're dependent on the earth. So we stay in a good frame of mind. It helps the winter go by, too, because I'm always thinking about spring. I want to get out in my garden and go to work. In the winter I sit and read the almanac and the gardening catalogs. It gives me something to talk to other people about. Lots of people garden around here, and we always have something to discuss

Jack: She's really energetic about it. Last winter she took my truck and loaded it down with manure from the neighbors. It was good for her garden, but my truck smelled for many days.

Bob: You seem to really enjoy the garden. What do you like best about the garden?

Beverly: I like working in the soil, seeing something grow, and the flavor of the vegetable. Food tastes better when it comes from my garden. I know where it comes from. I don't have to get it from a supermarket. It's a part of self-sufficiency. It's all tied up together. I enjoy sharing it with others. I give lots of produce away each summer. And I talk gardening with my friends, read about it, and read the almanac--all that kind of stuff. It's a way of life.

Bob: It's hard work though, isn't it?

Beverly: Yes, it is. Canning is done in the hottest month of the year--in August. We're busy with other things at that time of the year, too, so we really stay busy.

Jack: But it's good for you to work so hard. Hard work makes you healthy. To be self-sufficient you have to work hard and be healthy.

The challenge of the first year reminded families how much their lives had changed. Old routines were gone. Old acquaintances were missed. It was no longer possible to banter over a cup of coffee or discuss a decision with them. Often new friendships had not yet been made and, at times, the families were insufficient to meet the needs of their own members. Sometimes treasured new pleasures went unshared because there was no one to share them with. Moments of loneliness often crept up unexpectedly. New patterns for daily activities developed slowly and often left family members feeling incomplete. Shopping areas, medical services, and recreational areas had to be found. But families met the new demands, and were satisfied with the results.

For most families money always seemed to be a problem. They were faced with the task of providing and stabilizing an income capable of supporting themselves. This could be precarious. They usually had some savings and equity from the house they sold. In addition most had lowered their expenses by several thousand dollars a year. Still, they discovered they needed sizeable sums of money to live in the Ozarks. Housing and land, while often less expensive than in other parts of the U.S., still were not cheap, and could deplete savings. Medical and dental expenses remained high and transportation costs often soared because living far away from a major town meant that every shopping trip was accompanied by a large gasoline bill. Families were forced to do with less. Many found they needed more money than they had anticipated.

Economically, farming was precarious because land and equipment were expensive and prices for commodities were low. When a family lived on a small farm, however, it was often possible to look to the farm to provide some additional income. Large enterprises, though, such as dairy or livestock farms, were seldom begun because of the large investment needed and the length of start-up time. But less lucrative, although more practical, possibilities did exist. Families considered one of the smaller enterprises of the Ozarks--horticultural products, feeder pig production, rabbits, or dairy goats. Those could be started with small sums of money and in a fairly short period of time a marketable commodity could be produced. However, since markets normally did not readily exist for horticulture products and small animals, these markets had to be developed. Meanwhile, enough income had to be produced to pay the mortgage and meet family needs.

Families found that adjusting was continuous, but the challenge of the adventure usually allowed them to overcome the inconveniences they faced. The necessity for balancing small farm life with paid employment exerted a constant pressure. Many discovered they were working harder than they ever had in any previous job--and were enjoying it more. Consequently, most established themselves that first year.

CHAPTER VI

REFLECTION

About a year after their moves most people unexpectedly found they were wondering if the move had really been what they had wanted. This questioning or reflective period began just as they were beginning to feel confident and successful. The rural life which they had wanted and worked so hard to achieve was now part of them. Many believed that if they so chose, they could remain in the rural area for the rest of their lives. Therefore they were surprised that a period of questioning, which resulted in many returning to the urban area, crept back into their minds.

The reflective period, like the doubt that had proceeded it years earlier, also emerged from the unconscious parts of their minds. People discovered that in their frenzied activities to succeed, one of their major goals had not been met. Their activities had never abated. They had not slowed down or put the brakes on their lives. In fact, for most, quite the opposite had happened. People had been caught up in the challenge of the moves and, in their zeal to succeed, had necessarily speeded up.

But this was the situation they had hoped the moves would allow them to escape. They did not want to speed through life forever. They realized a need for a lull. Thoughts of stabilizing their lifestyles at a slower pace or returning to an urban area emerged. People found themselves questioning their original decisions to move. They wondered if the results of their activities had been worth their time and effort. And so, for yet another time, people had to think through many issues. It was again necessary to sort out, clarify, and establish the purposes of the moves. Once more they had to determine their personal preferences and the available alternatives, and whether or not they wanted to remain in the Ozarks.

There were many reasons for this reflective period. For some the desire to return to the city emerged because they had succeeded. These were highly industrious people who wanted and needed a challenge to inspire their efforts. Once they knew they could succeed, the challenge was gone. They knew they could stay, but much of the meaning of the move had dissipated. It was an ironic twist. With success, the impetus for their transition was lost.

A few became aware of personal problems like alcoholism, tenuous marriages, or lack of personal growth. People found that when they had prior problems, the moves delayed or sometimes even hid them for a while but seldom rectified their situations. The move was like the union of a marriage. Those who entered the moves in harmony found the country enriching, while those with personal problems found the moves complicated those problems.

> *This man remained in the Ozarks. But personal problems, which began years before he moved, surfaced after the move. It took several years for him to resolve many of these problems, but eventually he did so.*

> Ted: Even after we moved I still worked and worked and worked. I wanted us to succeed. I had my goals, too, and yet I never got to do the things I wanted to do. We

> never made progress on my goals. Then, I discovered I was drinking much too much. I was trying to kill myself, but drinking was too slow a way to die. I couldn't put myself out of my own misery. It just wasn't working. One day I was out working in the garden. I discovered I liked to do that. I hadn't realized before that I liked working in the garden. But once I knew that, things started changing. I started going to alcoholics anonymous. Other people started caring about me. And I got turned around. It was hard. I started making a gratitude list. Every day I learned to be grateful for something. At first it was just getting up in the morning. Then, I added more things to the list, everyday.

Others found that they had not been prepared for the full consequences of the move and had not made adequate preparation. They did not have enough money in reserves, and savings were quickly depleted. Farming skills took too long to develop. They could not find suitable jobs. Or, perhaps they did not even know how to go about looking for their first jobs--or better ones once initial employment was found. Often they found themselves mired in making decisions even when they knew they should be working toward their goals.

And, still others found their adjustments greater than they had imagined they would be. This was particularly true of those who made the greatest changes. Those who lowered their incomes the most found that they had to make the greatest adjustments. For instance, those who went from good urban jobs to attempts at total self-sufficiency on the farm found drastic changes. Often some of their needs for health, education, housing, and cultural events went unmet. The change from much to little was more than they could handle. Finding satisfactory friends and community support to replace the materialism they had known was not accomplished easily.

For nearly everyone money was a pervading issue. Seldom was there enough. And, though people were not surprised, the shortage contributed to their discouragement. Housing, clothing, transportation, and health costs often remained high. Few were able to be as self-reliant as they had hoped. Some could not maintain their incomes at what they felt were satisfactory levels. Their economic needs impaired their ability to enjoy life. Those who had an insufficient amount of money often made the decision to return to an urban area.

Here is how one couple made the decision to return to urban life.

Elaine: We have learned how to live on a small farm. We've eaten well and we haven't lost our health. But I really miss the things that made our society a pleasure.

Bob: Are you glad you came?

Elaine: It was great, especially when we first came. But now, with the money so hard to get we'll have to leave.

Bob: Is this the reason you are leaving?

Henry: Yes! Money is the main reason we are leaving. It's because I don't want to work for the rest of my life and not have anything. That's why I'm leaving. I'll go somewhere else, put my nose to the grindstone, and sixteen years from now I'll have a little nest egg. If I stayed here I would have to work for the rest of my life--until the day I died, and still not have anything.

Hardly anyone escaped this reflective period. For only a rare few was the move completed so quickly and satisfactorily that they never contemplated returning. Some were so ready to leave they could not consider staying, and others felt trapped and remained against their wishes. For most, the decision required additional thought and the balancing of desires against resources and possibilities.

But most who made the decision to return, believed their stay in the rural area had been worthwhile. They had met many of their own goals, learned more about themselves, and significantly increased their abilities. They were satisfied with what they had done. Only a few regretted the effort, and most were quick to label the move successful even when they did return. Their life in the rural area left an indelible imprint.

This family lived in a remote part of the Ozarks. Much to my surprise when I arrived at their home to conduct this interview the husband had already found employment in an urban area and left. His wife, whom I interviewed, was in the process of selling the farm so that she and their children could join her husband. They were disappointed with the educational opportunities available to their children and the lack of family income. Chapter XIII is devoted exclusively to her experiences in the country.

Bob: Do you understand your own feelings better? Has that been affected?

Mary: Yes! I don't think we will ever look at things the same after having this experience. I think it has emphasized what we have always felt. It has made it more real for us. In a philosophical way we have always felt people have got to learn how to survive. This just emphasized it even more.

Bob: So many of your feelings are the same as when you came?

Mary: Yes. We have had a lot of romantic ideas busted. And I think if it were just Jim and me, we would stay. In fact, I'm sure we would.

Bob: I don't get the feeling you think you have failed here. You don't view it that way, do you?

Mary: No, not at all. I think that's important for us. If we were failing, we would have stayed. I know we would have because I can't think of anything we've really ever failed at. We'd just keep plugging away until we succeeded. We would stay if we were failing. Definitely! But we knew we could have made it. It just was not what we had hoped it would be.

CHAPTER VII

PERMANENCE

For several years, those who remained found that their activities revolved around additional ways to support and sustain their new lifestyles. Initial decisions which were made the first year concerning personal actions, family activities, and community services gradually became daily routines. The time spent making those decisions became free time and was diverted to other uses. Of course, there were still some difficult decisions to make. People wanted to learn more about community life, visit with their neighbors, make new friends, and join social groups. Nevertheless, one of the major reasons for the move was to be able to do less instead of more. But, the first year had reinforced the need to be busy. So, people consciously had to decide to slow down. This was not an easy thing to do. For, as the in-migrants discovered, their own fast-paced lives conflicted with the slower pace that prevailed in the Ozarks.

This husband and wife raised their children in the Ozarks. This interview was held at a kitchen table. Catherine, particularly, had found 'slowing down' difficult. The family had lived in the Ozarks for ten years when this interview took place.

Bob: What did you expect here?

Dale: I expected a slowed down version of the city; I don't think I expected it to be quite as slow as it is.

Catherine: Well, I had never lived in the country. This slow down that was great for him was traumatic for me. Really, the first year we were here, I didn't see how people could possibly live and work under these conditions. If you had an appliance break down, you might as well plan on waiting to get it fixed. If the fellow felt like fixing it that day, he might. But if not, maybe he would fix it three days later.

Dale: She is saying that the biggest problem we had was getting used to the 'When we get around to it,' attitude--which I now like. But at that time we were not geared for it.

Catherine: And it was even harder, in my opinion, for a female. I usually took care of all the odd jobs. He went to work everyday and I took care of the insurance, money, the bills, and all that kind of stuff. It was a divided thing. When we moved here it quickly became apparent that these people, although they were very nice, were not used to dealing with a woman. They wanted to deal with him. If I had anything break down, I had very little luck calling someone to fix it. If I had him call, it would be taken care of in a shorter time. We acquired different kinds of livestock when we got here. I like to work with stock. But if there were questions with the stock and I needed answers, they were not complete. If he asked the farmers a question, we would get an answer that explained what we were doing. If I asked the question, it was, 'Do it like I say because you are supposed to.' I had a bad time with that. It just wasn't my thing. I wasn't used to doing things that way.

Bob: You certainly deserved to be treated as an equal!

Catherine: Well, I didn't even expect equalization! Just a little bit of common courtesy would have helped. But the adjustment was really hard for me.

Bob: What else was difficult?

Catherine: It was just so slow. I don't really think I lived a fast pace in Seattle. We entertained a lot there, but we do that here.

Bob: Did you find you were in conflict with others?

Catherine: No, he doesn't have that trouble. He never has had that trouble. He grew up in the country. He likes to sit and visit with people. To spend two hours talking to somebody to get something done doesn't bother him. If I am killing a day and want to spend two hours visiting with somebody, that's fine. If I have something I want done... If it's a business matter that needs to be taken care of, he usually does it instead of me. But I can watch the countryside change, and it has changed a lot. I can call a repair man now and get something done. When we came here, we moved out of a large home into a two bedroom trailer. That was hard for me. All of our belongings had to be stored. All the things that we had acquired and lived with over a ten year span went into storage because we didn't have any place to put them.

So we didn't really need to bring them with us, anyway. They weren't any good after that. After you're here for a while, you learn to relax. You also learn that you didn't need all that stuff that you brought with you. After that point, the adjustment is easy. I don't miss any of that stuff any more.

Bob: You have slowed down. Is that what you're telling me?

Catherine: Oh! Sure! I spend days wasting time now. And enjoy it. I wouldn't live any place else.

Slowing down was crucial to becoming loving, giving, and caring. And, to fully realize that potential, many had to complete the journey into themselves. It was difficult to concentrate on doing less instead of more. Some felt guilty for not allowing old thoughts of success to dominate. Others found that past tensions were hidden and locked in the mind and were now surfacing as uninvited emotions begging for attention. But for the most part, people found that they had to replace old aggressive behavior with love, kindness, and caring. To do this many concentrated on finding satisfaction in their current tasks. Slowly, they began to discover a more peaceful way of life.

During this time many reverted to the arts and crafts which they had earlier fostered but had found insufficient time to continue during their first years. People regained their skills as woodworkers, musicians, dancers, potters, leatherworkers, and seamstresses. This same of creative endeavor paralleled other everyday activity. People continued to strive to be self-reliant. They still found a tremendous amount of satisfaction on the small farm and in the gardens which they grew. They were pleased to be in a natural setting away from the man-made objects of an urban life. And, they spent time with family and friends. They shared daily events, talked about the past, and found time to dream about tomorrow.

This short excerpt came from a father who had developed many mechanical skills. He had a small shop and became the neighborhood "handyman." He believed his diverse abilities would allow him to become self-sufficient.

Bob: What are you attempting to do here?

George: We're trying to become as self-sufficient as possible.

Bob: What is it to be self-sufficient?

George: We're trying to make a living without ever having to leave this community if we don't want to. We're trying to raise our own food, barter with the neighbors, and just work for friends doing things they need done. That's how we get our money. Being self-sufficient means to do as much as possible by yourself, or with family and friends.

People were changing. Meaning in their lives was coming from a new direction. No longer was the job, employment, or success in material goods so important. Rather the love, hope, sharing, and giving which they had wanted to foster was now finding expression. People were incorporating their inner needs in their everyday activities. But this could not be accomplished alone. People had not changed their lifestyles in a vacuum removed from others and they certainly could not find adequate enrichment only from within. To continue to feel sustained and grow, people found that they had to look beyond themselves--into community life--for the kind of help which they needed.

COMMUNITY LIFE

One of the major introductions which people received to community life came when they needed public services. For, usually, a difference existed between public services in the rural and urban areas and adjustments had to be made. For example, one of the things which people quickly found attractive about rural life was the fact that taxes, particularly property taxes, were almost always lower. But, tax-payers received fewer services, too. And this lower level of services was often diminished even more by the fact that people often built their homes scattered along roads and highways rather than congregating them in small towns and cities. This dispersal made services more difficult as well as more costly. When this was coupled with a large influx of people, services were often delayed.

This lack of public services was often first noticeable when people discovered they were personally responsible for drilling their own wells and building their sewage treatment facilities. When people constructed new homes in rural areas, these facilities added significantly to the cost. And when they purchased an older home, the facilities had to be maintained. Small towns often do not provide one or both of these services. And there were other contrasts to their previous residences, too. Usually there was an absence of building codes and zoning regulations in the rural areas. While most people enjoyed the personal freedom from any restrictions, they occasionally resented the building styles, land abuse, and groundwater contamination such freedom allowed. Others could build substandard housing and sell it as they desired. Roads, too, offered a sharp contrast to urban areas. Construction and maintenance standards were not comparable to urban areas. Vast miles of roadways were often rough, rocky, and unpaved. They wore down automobiles quicker and, when car repair costs were coupled with fuel costs associated with long distances between services and destinations, the cost of transportation escalated. Perhaps the most startling difference in public services centered on fire protection and ambulance services. These rural services were normally made up of volunteers who gave their time to train and respond to requests for emergency help. People found that an emergency had to wait for a crew to assemble and make the run. Fires in homes and buildings located even short distances from fire stations often did extensive damage; and heart attacks and serious automobile accidents occurred far from the nearest hospital. Emergencies were occasions when there was a tremendous amount of anxiety and occasional tragedy. People had to become much more aware and accepting of the possibility of a tragedy striking them or someone they loved.

Here's the answer of one family which responded to the question 'what's it like to live in the country?'

Marge: If you have never lived in the country you get used to a different type of house, maybe a water system that's not right, a telephone that goes out if the weather is really damp... I think it's learning to do without. You cannot plan like you can in the city. I've learned to shop once a month because of the time it takes to drive back and forth. Where we formerly lived if we had a sick child and needed a prescription filled on Sunday afternoon, it was no problem to get one. Here you learn not to need a

> drugstore past 5:00 on Saturday afternoon. If you are in the city and your car breaks down, your neighbor next door is going to have one or you can call a cab, take a bus, or whatever. Here if your car breaks down, you walk. There's no mechanic nearby! If you make a doctor's appointment, you spend an hour and a half to three hours just getting there. It takes that long to go to Springfield. In the city there are so many people and services available that you don't worry. If you can't get in to see one doctor, you know of another. Here if your child is ill there are usually only one or two local doctors available. If your child is particularly healthy and hasn't been to a doctor for years and then gets sick, any previous doctor has probably moved. There's a turnover here.

In their quest for public services people joined existing groups or helped form new organizations. Water, fire, ambulance, and sewer districts proliferated with the influx of people. But these quasi-governmental agencies were not the only organizations that sprang to life. Social and recreational groups such as churches, little league baseball, sportsmen's clubs, service groups, and craft guilds also came into existence. And, with the formation of each group, another outlet for expressing the social life of the community came into existence. For, not only did the groups provide needed services, but they allowed new members to meet other community residents, make friends, and learn more about their new community. Organizations allowed people to both contribute and receive from the community in which they resided. And, groups helped support the new lifestyles they were building.

At times, though, the groups found themselves in conflict and dissension. There was conflict between groups for limited money and competing ideas, or strife within groups for positions of leadership. Other problems arose when groups became efficient and effective. Their success began to change the social order of the community--a process which often stirred up even more antagonisms. Sometimes the migrants were surprised that disagreements would ever develop. Some believed, for a while, that the dissension was of recent vintage until they heard stories about small towns and rural areas and discovered that even the sleepiest of rural areas had long histories of rivalry between groups, organizations, and families. The new residents remembered that the urban areas they had come from experienced contention among political, economic, and social groups. This present conflict was often only a continuation of older disputes. Sometimes it even infused vigor into community life as neighbors sought creative ways to resolve their differences. And, while at times the disputes were detrimental and hurtful, they did not prevail; rather, cooperation and self-help eventually dominated. People learned to work together to solve community problems. And in so doing, they found a place to grow, change, and gain support in their everyday activities.

Finally, many expressed the desire for the area to remain as it was. People recognized the dilemma that as people moved to the Ozarks, the area changed from what it had been. And yet, this was what most wanted to avoid. They wanted the area to remain as it was without change except for their own presence. Some expressed the belief that they had found heaven and now wanted the gate closed behind them to keep others out.

This mother was caught in the tension of wanting both a better, faster-paced, and more stimulating life for her children and the slow tradition-steeped culture of the Ozarks. This tension is expressed here in terms of the school system and the education which the young people received. She had lived in the area for several years and two of her children were in high school while three others had already graduated.

Helen: I doubt that I could have made this move without the ten years in Minneapolis. I think you have to be in a certain state of mind before you are ready to settle in an area like this. I don't think most young people can. I think you have to be ready for this area before you move here and that's why many people don't stay. I don't blame the young people for moving away. There's nothing for them to do. They're not ready to sit outside and look at the lake for hours at a time. They have to have something to do. This area is not going to give them that for some time.

Look around! It's not young people moving here. It's middle aged and older people. People who are ready for something beside hurrying every place they go. There won't be any young people moving here for a long time unless things in the city get so tight they can't find any place else to live. They wouldn't opt to live here without having tried something else first, it seems to me.

I don't begrudge any of the time we spent in the city. We had to live there first to learn what it had to give. There are still things that I miss. I miss it for my kids; let's put it that way. There aren't the cultural advantages here that had been down the street where they lived.

I think that's one thing here the parents really have to work at; to get their children out of this area--not move them out--but allow them to travel out to learn. This area does not allow the children to learn the customs of other people. These kids go away to college and an integrated school system and I think they're at a disadvantage when they do. They're not ready if they've not traveled outside of this school system.

How many of the kids in this area have ridden on a city bus? Or taken a taxi? Or train? Have seen an ethnic neighborhood? Have seen the ocean? These kids grow up, become eighteen, graduate from high school, and are ready to meet the world but have been no where. Most of them stumble around in it and survive. I'm not saying anything against the school system. They try to teach. But, when this child goes to an urban area, maybe he will find a job, sure! But, they also have to find a place to live, contact all the utility companies, have a phone, and do all the average everyday things that have to be done. They have to do them with people who are different than the people they've grown up with. It's different. These aren't people who are going to sit down and talk with you two hours before putting a phone in your house. No! They don't know how to talk to others, and others don't know how to talk to them. So, the education that they receive is only good in this area.

They run into social problems they've never run into before. The kids who grow up and stay here through their eighteenth year have no idea why a child in another part of the country is rioting or why they are demanding more. They don't know. They have no idea. If a kid isn't allowed to travel outside of this area, then to me he is deprived. This area doesn't intend to deprive its kids, but its a fact of life that it does. I worry about the kids who live here and go away. Say they move to Chicago and go to college..or New York, or Los Angeles. These kids would be at such a terrible disadvantage. They would not only have the cultural shock of moving out of the Ozarks and learning to live on their own, but they would have the cultural shock of learning to live with people who are different.

I'm sure that for the most part they have the best education that this area can give them, but they're not educated socially. Not at all. I don't know how to change that. It won't change for a lot of years--especially when people like us move here because this area is slower and more leisurely. We try hard to keep it the way it is so that it won't change. So, our kids have a continual hassle.

FRIENDSHIP

People recognized that nothing added more meaning to their moves than the friendships which they made. They believed that the quality of life could best be enhanced by knowing and interacting with others. Only through others could their lives be sustained and renewed. While economic stability and community participation were important, they did not insure the success of new lifestyles. Only personal interaction could do that.

It took several years for this family to complete their transition before arriving at this successful conclusion .

Pat: We've always had a house that had space for others in it. It may not have been a big house, but if we shifted people around we could fit people in. We are really lucky here in the fact that we've got the extra room. There are many weeks that we have company for dinner four or five nights out of the week. Well, I say company. There is someone here but they are not really company. I like that. I enjoy my private life. And I enjoy being by myself,

> but on the other side of it I enjoy a house full of people, too. There's a time when you need to be by yourself. I wouldn't enjoy a continually empty house. I enjoy being with people and I enjoy seeing how they live, too. Many people, like I said, come and go from here and have a different lifestyle than we do. It makes it possible for us to see the way they live and enjoy the way they live. It works out well for me. When our daughter was home for Thanksgiving she made the statement that if she had not lived in our house she would have missed out on a lot of unusual people. That was kind of neat.

People were encouraged when their first contacts with others were relatively easy to make. For, at first, similarities dominated. People were drawn together out of a mutual interest. There were contacts with a realtor, an employer, service people, and nearby neighbors. Normally everyone was kind, courteous, and considerate with each other.

But a lingering restlessness remained. Since the newcomers normally were not accustomed to rural ways and lacked the skills of rural people, they wondered if they would be accepted. They feared they might "stick out like a sore thumb." They wanted to be known and accepted for what they were becoming, not for what they had been. They needed encouragement and believed an informal atmosphere could best provide this support. And, almost always, the natives responded kindly. When people needed information about gardening, raising calves, or small-scale farming, there was a neighbor to help provide the information. Mutual curiosity of one for the other and overlapping interests prevailed. Strangers became acquaintances.

Nevertheless, there was nothing fast about making friendships. People found that after their initial acceptance, differences became more noticeable. The terms "native" and "newcomer" came into use. Often there was a cooling off in the relationship and a period to "wait and see" if the congeniality would continue.

At first the extent of the differences was difficult to discern. Some of the first revolved around the use of land. As people moved in, farms were often broken into smaller units rather than retained as large ones. More people had ownership and this helped push the price of land upward. Those who could afford land were those who moved in from outside the area. The "newcomers" were pricing "natives" out of the land market.

In addition, the use of that land often changed--particularly as it related to recreation uses and hunting rights. "Natives" had long ago established their recreational right to the land. They enjoyed hunting, fishing, and pursuing game. Yet, this was often altered when the "newcomers" moved in. In their zeal for conservation of soil, land, and game, the "new people" often "posted" their land which meant that they did not allow any hunting and fishing to take place. The intention was to conserve land and game--the effect often was to break up long-standing patterns which were practiced by the natives.

But it was often the lifestyle itself which perpetuated the differences between those who moved in and those who already lived in the rural areas. The natives had a lifestyle based on tradition, family relationships, friendships, and mutual interaction with others. They already knew their needs and how to farm or how to obtain assistance from family and friends. They had jobs or knew where employment could be found. Their support stemmed from living for generations in one place. Normally those who were moving in were looking for these qualities. The newcomers were learning how to gain this knowledge. They were experimenting; the native residents were stable. And often, the former urban residents had a planned escape route back to the city if they needed it. There was a cultural difference between the two groups. Is it any wonder that apprehensions sometimes lingered for years?

But those who struggled through years of uncertainty had reasons to be pleased. Friendship, kindness, and mutual support prevailed. Those who were new found that the close contacts which were possible in small communities were mutually sustaining. People came to know each other in a variety of ways. A grocer, banker, or mechanic could readily be one's neighbor and friend as well as the person on whom one relied for needed services. They could exchange their joy and happiness, struggles, anger, and disappointments. Those who were new became satisfied with their everyday activities and were sustained by those with whom they came in contact.

High winds blew the roof off this family's house. His neighbors banded together in an effort reminiscent of the neighborhood thrashing crew or barn raising of old and replaced the roof. It was a memorable experience for all concerned. Here is how the family told the story.

Wayne: The roof of my house is a good example. We live on top of the hill and get high winds. One night this summer, about three months ago, the whole front porch and half of my roof blew off. By 8:00 the next morning, without me calling anyone, people were on the roof surveying the damage. The only thing I did was call my neighbor when the roof went off, and we went over and stayed the night with them. I'm sure they started the ball rolling. We had threatening weather the first day they worked on the house. By dark we had the house built back to where it would be dry if it rained again. Nobody asked 'How much an hour am I going to make?' We had

> as many as ten people on that roof at one time. I drove in and loaded up a load of lumber and nails and whatever I needed and came back out here--this was on Sunday. I had called the lumber yard owner at home, and he said, 'Go down there and I will meet you.' We got the material and came back and started rebuilding. The lumber yard didn't ask me, 'When are you going to pay this bill?' I had carpenters. I had retirees. I had people from all walks of life carrying shingles, rafters, or whatever was needed. We had this place dried in. But they didn't quit when it got dried in. We rebuilt the porch. My insurance company said that I should replace the opposite side of the roof because the part that blew off had damaged the rest of the roof. After we got the house dried in and better weather arrived, these same neighbors came back and said, 'let's put the roof on.' And we put the roof on. The only thing they would accept for pay was that I took the whole crew out to dinner--the whole bunch that worked on the roof. They didn't take any pay and they worked for two days.

Yet, all who engaged in the process of changing their lifestyles eventually reached that time when they hoped the transition would come to an end. There were times when everyone grew tired of the change and the effort necessary to deal with the uncertainty of their futures. A few, in their more despondent moments, had grown tired of being tired. Even those who had passed through the smoothest and most successful transitions experienced times when they grew weary. But eventually for everyone, there was a time when continuity and repetitive action again began to characterize their everyday lives. The transition to change a lifestyle had drawn to a close. They were Ozark residents living a stable lifestyle.

STABILITY AGAIN

Almost everyone who stayed in the rural area declared that in the end they were pleased. The moves had ushered in dramatic changes and had made their lives vastly different. They were satisfied with themselves and the results of their moves. Many stated they would never again move. They had found all they could reasonably expect. Yet, many found success difficult to explain. Just as every case that comes before a judge in a courtroom differs, so everyone who had moved had a different story to tell about their own experiences. Common denominators were difficult to identify.

This family found greater security and relaxation as a part of their move.

Darlene: This part of the country allows you to relax. When you live in the city and financial times become harder than they are now, you either make it on your salary or you don't. You sink or swim. There is no in between. Here if things get harder most people could do without part of the things they are living with because social pressures don't demand that you have as much. You can have your garden and raise three-fourths of what you eat. You can hunt, raise calves, pigs, and chickens. Home grown food is an option now. We could depend on it if we had to. We have an option. In the city there isn't an option. I think that allows me to relax. Financial security, 'security' period, was always very important to us.

Bob: You can't starve to death here can you?

Darlene: You can't. Absolutely not. If you do it's laziness. If a person who has never lived in the country, had a garden, or raised an animal could move here and learn to do it, and I did, then anyone can. Max went to work everyday. Someone had to take care of the animals. I know I can raise a garden and care for animals.

Max: The people here have a barter system. If I raise chickens and have eggs and the man across the way wants to raise a garden and grow tomatoes, then we can trade. In the time we've been here, I've participated in it. Our neighbor bought a tractor and I maintain it. We both use it.

Bob: That's barter.

Darlene: It allows you to relax. You don't have to fight. If you know you are not going to starve and your kids are going to be comfortable, you can afford to relax. You know you can do without if you ever have to.

Many were particularly pleased when they compared their present with what they thought they would have become if they had stayed in an urban area. Some envisioned what they might have become and others went back to the urban area during vacations to visit old friends. Many did not like what they saw. They were much more pleased with what they had become.

Here are further comments by Max and Darlene.

Darlene: We were here six years before we went back to visit the place he worked. It was startling. And, I don't think six years is a long time if you're established in a good job. But, over fifty percent of the people he worked with were gone. Most of them were dead, not just transferred to another job.

Max: For example, one man who had a very good work record had been killed by his son. He had tried to intervene in a fight and his son hit him over the head with a pop bottle and killed him. I had a paint man who was two years from retirement and he hung himself in the garage at home. Another person turned into an alcoholic. Pressures got to them. To this day I bet there are not two left in the company. I figure I would have been one of the deaths if I had stayed.

Still others had moved to the rural area in hopes of hastening retirement--of not having to wait until those retirement years came around so that they could live and fill their own hours with the activities that they preferred.

This young man was alive and alert and extremely excited when he blurted out:

Larry: See, other people talk about retirement and what they'll do when they retire. I've had my retirement--and had it when I was young enough to enjoy it. It was great. I don't have to look forward to retirement now. I've done it--and I'm doing it daily. We don't have much money and I'm not sure what we'll be doing in a few years, but I have confidence we can do it.

One of the discoveries many made was that in their quest to simplify their lifestyles they seldom cut down on their activities. Even years after the move they were amazed at how busy they remained. They still went places, did things, and filled up their time with activities. Yet, they were satisfied. Simplicity did not mean inaction. They enjoyed going to school functions, civic and organizational meetings, and churches, and they enjoyed meeting friends and neighbors on the streets and in stores. Simplicity gave a greater fullness and depth to these activities. They appreciated the neighborliness which existed in the rural areas. Their lives took on the meaning of people who were mutually supporting and sustaining.

The simplification had more to do with their internal lives than with any outward manifestation. Time spent in introspection had been productive. Many acknowledged a stronger recognition of their own uniqueness, found greater distinctions between themselves and others, and considered alternatives which they had never before comprehended. They had developed their potential. The inward strength which they sought had emerged.

> *The loving, giving, and caring which many wanted to develop also emerged. Many learned to give more than they ever had before. For some the caring showed through in family life, while for others their love was exhibited in their employment.*
>
> Catherine: I'd say that each other and the family are our highest priorities. That's more important than all the assets a person can have.
>
> Dale: We've decided that rather than spend all our time acquiring things for the future, we would enjoy what we

have right now. We're sure the future will work itself out. As long as we're happy, we seem to work out the future without planning for it. If we're unhappy, then problems that might arise are larger than they need to be. We're just getting younger instead of older.

Bob: You're enjoying it here?

Dale: You bet. And I'm happier now than I've ever been in my life! Either that or I'm not smart enough to know the difference. Whatever! It's great.

This teacher discussed the changes that had taken place in her life since she had moved. Earlier she had told me that she had become a much more religious person since her move.

Bob: Are there any other areas in which you've grown?

Jean: Caring about people. When I was a full-time language teacher [before the move] I knew that I had the cream of the crop in my classes. Kids who take language are in the upper quarter of their class. If they aren't, they don't take foreign language very long. So, I knew that I had top-notch kids. And I was very grateful that I didn't have to deal with anybody that was less than top-notch. It was a very snobby attitude on my part.

Now, I help teach children who need special education classes. My heart goes out to each of the kids. One in particular is caught in a family struggle and I am positive that has a great effect on the way he is right now. I think that with the atmosphere of the school where I teach now we can help him work it out and he can be a productive human being. It's exciting for me. That's like somebody going out and building a monument or building or something from the ground up. You hear of people around here who go out and grow the timber, cut it themselves, saw it into boards, make their own nails, do their own plumbing, do their own architectural drawings, and build the house from the ground up. They are excited about it. They are proud that the house is built that way. I feel that way about these kids. I know that I participate in what will ultimately be--a little piece of eternity. And it's awesome.

Time and again people related how they had grown, changed, become more perceptive, or developed personal attributes. Many described a reduction in tension, more peace and happiness, satisfaction with family and friends, and greater enjoyment with their employment and leisure activities. Others discovered that "doing nothing" could be meaningful. They wanted to talk about what they had learned but had to struggle to express the importance of the experience. It seemed they were attempting to relate a part of themselves that they could feel, were in some way sensitive to, but could not find.

In an attempt to identify this "unknown" aspect which people referred to, I finally asked one man this question.

Bob: Could this move to the country be considered a spiritual odyssey?

Lyle: Yes, that's a good word for it. People are growing in all the ways that affect their expressive lives. They are evolving in ways that connect them to the fundamental and enduring parts of our world. Things in our culture

> come and go, but values, ethics, and even mysticism remain. I think that many people move because they want to learn more about this part of themselves that they know so little about. For some it's God, but for many it's just a knowledge of the unknown.

Emotional and rational needs blended as they had not done before. People became attuned to new rhythms. The earth, growing things, weather, and the seasons became discernable influences and heightened the belief of many in a supreme being. They were more in step with others and themselves.

And yet, even though their lives were marked by stability, not all change ceased. People continued to grow older and to change with the seasons. Families changed, communities changed, conditions around them changed, their own values changed. But change transformed itself into growth and self-renewal. People viewed life as an expansion of potential rather than as an oppressive stalemate. Many found they had enhanced their ability to anticipate and even bring about change. Most learned to accept both their present and whatever the future might be.

Perhaps, though, the greatest change in their lives was the realization that they were back in control of their own destinies. They had generated meaning in their daily existence and were primarily responsible for their own accomplishments. They had participated in the creation of their own lifestyle--and they had been successful.

Chapter VIII

RETURN TO THE URBAN LIFE

This chapter contains one of the first interviews I conducted. Mary, the woman I interviewed, was extremely perceptive about herself and the community in which she lived. She and her husband had already decided to leave the area when we talked. In the interview she talks about those reasons. But she also felt that she and her family had been successful. They had experienced another way of living.

Bob: Why don't you tell me a little bit about yourself?

Mary: O.K. I was raised in Harrisonville, Missouri until I was a teenager. Then our family moved to Arizona. Jim was raised in Minnesota. We met in Wisconsin and married there. We've been married fourteen years. He graduated from school and joined the ATC corporation. He was a salesman for them.

Bob: The school was where?

Mary: Wisconsin. I did not graduate but he did. I worked and he went through. Typical story. Then we moved all over the country with ATC. Mainly we were on the East Coast which we did not like. The final move was to Baltimore which was rather disastrous for us. We simply didn't like it. It was terrible weather, and we found that we didn't like that large of a city. I was not raised in a rural situation at all although my grandparents lived on a farm and I visited them all the time and I loved the farm. Jim really wasn't either although he was raised in small towns. But our interest just sort of evolved that way. We've always been very crafty, very interested in all kinds of crafts. And Jim, of course, has been pretty much involved in woodwork. We've always wanted to garden and raise animals. We began about five years ago talking about homesteading of some sort. We were preparing ourselves for the day when we could do that.

Bob: Did you raise animals?

Mary: No, we did not raise any animals. We were not in a situation where we could. But we did have a small garden. We were learning by reading. We got *Organic Gardening* and *Mother Earth News.* We picked up every how-to book we could find and just read about doing things. We became more and more involved in trying to homestead. Also, I became very involved in the World Hunger Program. I gave seminars and workshops on hunger. Our family began to eat more nutritionally, to be more interested in good food, in how to limit our meat consumption, and those kinds of things. We learned how to eat cheap.

Bob: What was Jim's job? Can you be more specific on this?

Mary: When he started he was a salesman. He sold industrial chemicals, not insect sprays or anything like that. We were living in Atlanta when he was transferred to Baltimore. In Baltimore he was regional distribution manager which meant he sold to other distributors in the region, which included Maryland, Pennsylvania, New Jersey, and Delaware.

Bob: What about the job? Was there anything in particular Jim did not like about it?

Mary: Yes, during his whole career, which had been eight or nine years, Jim had been the sole man in his office. He had no boss directly over him. Baltimore was the first situation where he was in a regional office where there were several salesmen and a boss. If he and his boss had hit it off right, things might have been different. But he and his boss were just two different personalities and that made it difficult. At the same time, as I said before, we were going through this wanting to be more self-sufficient, more involved, and that kind of thing. It just hit at the right time.

Bob: You felt claustrophobia with the job and the city?

Mary: Yes, the hassle of the city, the commuting, and being surrounded by neighbors. Although we had a lot of friends, we didn't necessarily have a great deal in common with them because they were getting ahead, buying new cars, this kind of thing that we just...

Bob: You had severe doubts about it?

Mary: Yes, we had just never been oriented toward spending money. We've always lived below our means and we just were never into all that. I mean, we always bought old furniture and fixed it up. We have never eaten a lot of steak. We've never been great consumers, really. I don't know why. We live in an age where it's all right to be experimental with life.

We always took a vacation but we never went to big, fancy resorts. We never consumed all that we could afford. Jim was raised rather poor. I was a minister's daughter but we weren't church mice; I mean, poor-poor. I was not raised to want things.

I guess we felt somewhat like an outsider in the city atmosphere with our own peer group. We felt that since we were in our early thirties and our children were young, that now was the time to try it.

It was still rather vague a year ago as to where we would go or what we would do. We went to Jim's parents a year ago for a vacation and passed through the Ozarks for the very first time in our lives. We said, 'Hey, this is beautiful. It's really nice.' We wanted to be somewhere where there were trees in a secluded spot. We read an ad in the *Mother Earth News* that there was a place down here. We decided at Christmas time we would come down. We did and we drove up to this place and said that was it. We were scared to death. Are we really going to do this? So we didn't make the deal. We went home and thought about it for a month. We knew we couldn't hack living there any more after we had been here for that week. We just had to try. We were just ready. So we did. Everybody thought that we were absolutely nuts--from our families to everybody.

Bob: How did you tell people?

Mary: Well, we just told them. We said, 'Hey, we're going to do this.' We really had not talked too much to people outside our family about ever doing this so everyone was pretty well shocked that we had ever considered it. Most businessmen that Jim told, because he had to tell them, envied and admired him for trying it. Several made comments like 'I wish I had tried it years ago, but now I can't,' that kind of thing. For a lot of people, though, it was 'Well, it's not for me but I admire you for trying.' But people were very interested in knowing how it went. They wanted us to correspond and let them know how things were going. Of course, the people in the hunger program were very interested.

Bob: What were the reactions of your families?

Mary: My family thought we were nuts starting at the beginning and all the way through. My father is not living now but my brother is a teacher and my sister is a sculptress. We are a very diverse family. They are very academic and doers in the sense they want to have hobbies. Jim's family was very supportive. Of course, they came from a more rural background.

Bob: How many acres do you have here?

Mary: Twenty-five.

Bob: What were your plans? To make a living on twenty-five acres or?

Mary: No. The plan was to raise all our own food except for things like mayonnaise or potato chips or whatever we couldn't grow. And, Jim was going to develop a woodworking business. One of the main points in doing this was that Jim and I would be together. That was one thing I neglected to mention earlier. He had had to travel during his entire career. That meant he was away from home at least two nights a week for seven years. Often he was gone four nights a week. So, we wanted to find a situation where we could be together and work as a team at something. This seemed like the ideal situation.

Bob: Let's break this conversation into two parts. Tell me first what went well and then let's talk about what was not successful.

Mary: O.K. We did raise all our own food. That part of this experience worked beautifully. It's the hardest work that we have ever done. And it was very frustrating work. But it was successful. We raised animals and we butchered them. We had rabbits and we had hogs and chickens. And, we raised the garden.

Bob: Did you raise your own hogs? I mean you had a sow and...?

Mary: Yes, we had a sow and a boar.

Bob: You had little pigs and raised them?

Mary: No, she was barren. One in ten thousand or something like that. We butchered her and sold him and he paid for all the feed so it worked out fine.

Bob: And you found the gardening to be more than you thought it would be?

Mary: Yes, but it was much harder because there had not been a garden on this plot of ground for years and it was sod. Someone before us had planted grass and fed animals on it. We got here with no equipment, no tractor--nothing. We assumed there would be a farmer nearby with a plow who would plow it. It turns out nobody cultivates land here. They're livestock farmers and they all have tractors but no plows. It was a frustration getting it plowed. We did most of it by hand. Planting the garden was not a big problem, but a half an acre is a large garden. It was more than we had ever done before. We had raised gardens before but only small city gardens and just for my pleasure of growing things and eating them fresh during the summer. But now, it was a different story. Now, it was 'This produces or we don't eat.'

That was a whole different feeling. The weather was so much more important. Get it in and get it up between rains and before the heat or summer--that whole thing. We had never had to anticipate how much we needed.

Bob: How did you preserve?

Mary: I canned.

Bob: Had you canned before?

Mary: No, I had never canned before. It was something new. We were city people. I canned so much and the constant concern was whether it would be enough to get us through the winter. And, it had to be done in the August heat. One of the things I hadn't anticipated was how much I'd miss the central air conditioning we had always had. We had very supportive friends here who helped us a great deal. Up and down the road here there are several older ladies who have lived here forever. They know when to put the beans in and this kind of thing--it was great.

Bob: And they were willing to share?

Mary: Yes. Very much so! Then, of course, having Jim here was great. The experience was terrific for our marriage, the real partnership out there of sweating it out together. And it was the same with the animals. Neither of us had ever raised animals before. Again, it was a situation where our grandparents had been on a farm and we had enjoyed it as children but we had never had the responsibility of doing it. We went dashing in the house to read what to do next. Now, if we raised hogs again we'd know what to do. I'm sure people laughed at us.

Bob: It had its moments of fun?

Mary: Yes, it was fun for us. We were very busy and tired of it, but it was a pleasurable experience.

Bob: What else went well?

Mary: The children.

Bob: What about the children?

Mary: It was an enormously great experience for the children. They had never seen a live chicken or live hog. They hadn't ever had any of these experiences. They were lonely here, but they really learned to do for themselves and carry some responsibilities. It has been fun for them.

Bob: And you have how many children?

Mary: Three.

Bob: And their ages?

Mary: Nine, six, and two. Mary Ann is the oldest. She thinks about things like going out at night with the telescope and seeing the stars and talking and learning about the stars. The animal life has been interesting for them and we have taken time to observe it. This is the first time their father has had a chance to be really involved in their lives all day long. So that was a fantastic experience for them.

Bob: O.K. Things that didn't go well?

Mary: That was the woodworking. We had hoped to get into making fine custom-made furniture. We started out in the craft shows as a way to bring in some income. But that was a general disappointment. First of all, we found that at craft shows people are not interested in really fine things. They are interested in little novelties which we just did not want to get into. So the sales did not go well. Secondly, the income level in this area is so low that people cannot afford and are not interested in well made furniture. The retired people who have moved here are generally in situations where they have sold off most of their belongings and now reside in smaller dwellings or in trailers. They don't want new furniture at all. And as I say, the income level of long-time residents is such that they cannot afford nice things. We thought before we got here that since this is a tourist area this would be a good situation for it. It wasn't. It just didn't bring in much. We did a poor job of anticipating sales. A lot of people in the area brought things for Jim to refinish. But there is no money in refinishing. In the cities they charge a great deal, but not here. People just cannot afford it. So Jim did refinish several things but he did not make anything. And, as I say, the whole aim was to get into fine furniture because for Jim making one of something is fun but making fifty is a drag. That was why he didn't want to get into novelties or anything that was an assembly line project. When he had to go to that, it was no fun for him. It just wasn't what he wanted.

Bob: He's a very creative person?

Mary: Yes, very.

Bob: He has the skill for making furniture?

Mary: Oh yes. He's made a lot of furniture. It was not a matter of skill. We consigned things to a shop in Springfield and it all sold. There again, maybe if we had waited it out, the woodworking would have eventually developed into a business. But, because we needed the income we would never have been able to get away from having to do these craft shows which was not what Jim wanted. You see, the people in the craft shows travel all over the country. Well, here we go! We're back in the same situation if he does that. Daddy's traveling.

No, if he had to be involved in that situation we might as well go back and make some money. So, at that point it didn't matter that it would be a long time or maybe never that he could make a sufficient income. That was when we decided that he should get a job.

Bob: He worked part-time, didn't he?

Mary: Well, he continued to do the woodworking but he worked full time for a small town. He was supervisor of their home energy crew for two months. But this, again, was another thing that did not work out. Jim had to drive forty-five minutes to work everyday. The town did not have a truck for him so he had to use our truck for his job. It was loaded with gear for working on homes. He learned a great deal about energy conservation and weatherizing homes. It was a good experience in that sense. He's always been interested in energy conservation and building. But, he got minimum wage. So, by the time he drove to work and used our truck, which had to have a new engine put in at our expense, we ended up losing money by him having that job. If the truck hadn't broken down, we could have supported ourselves at the minimum wage. In the long run, we could have survived here with Jim having a job at local wages. But that's because we have the food, and he's handy as a plumber and an electrician. We were doing almost everything ourselves so expenses were minimal.

Bob: What is your general sense or feeling about the experience and about leaving the area?

Mary: We learned more than we could have learned in a lifetime living in the city. We learned about ourselves, about how far we can stretch and grow, and how many frustrations we can cope with before we break. We know how well we can adapt to a situation that was virtually foreign to us except through reading about it. We learned about nature and a greater sense of where we as humans fit into nature.

Bob: You feel like you have grown?

Mary: Very, very much so. All of us have. I've more of a sense of who I am and my ability as a human being to function at a very basic level. It's things that you never think about living in the city. You go to the grocery store and buy your food. Income is a check. Your husband doesn't really work that hard and you don't either. You push papers and you get a check. There is no real sense of what that income is or what it means to you. There is no sense of survival. I've discovered I feel very different about paying cash for food and growing it myself.

We had to pack our own household completely. That was something we had never done before. There was a blizzard the day we started packing and forty inches of snow on the ground the day we left Baltimore. When we left, we hired a college boy to drive one of the trucks for us. He had never driven a truck before. It took us six days to make a two and a half day trip because at some point every vehicle broke down. One day we counted twenty-three jack knifed semi-trailers on the road. We finally left the truck in Indiana. We were freezing. It was just one thing piled on another. The whole time we wondered if we were going to survive. Once we arrived, it was too muddy to get to the house. We had to wait three days to get up here. When we did, we couldn't get back down. We had no food and no heat--nothing. It was bitter cold. We began to say, 'Are we going to survive today?' We were unloading the van and found a bag of potatoes and one onion. We cooked that and ate it. We finally killed a chicken that was around here and put it in the pot for the next meal and it wasn't too bad. But we did not get out. We had no phone and no heat. We wondered, 'what do you do?' We learned how to survive. We were not able to talk about it at the time because we both felt that if we sat down and talked we might fall apart. We just kept going in order to get through that one day because the following day would be better. We just made one mechanical move after another to get through it. We had three children. We were cold and hungry and it was all new. We had to get through it. Nothing has ever been quite as bad as that.

Bob: Good way to start in, isn't it?

Mary: Yes, we figured everything had to be up hill from there. Another, briefer situation happened a couple of weeks ago when it was pouring rain. I got stuck in the middle of the creek. The creek was running very fast. Here, again, was a situation where I had to be very calm. The car was filling up with water so I had to get out. I honestly feared for my life if I got out of the car. I was afraid I was going to be washed down the creek. It was that kind of mechanical thing again. 'How am I going to get out of here? How am I going to remain calm and make it across.' Those are situations that you just never run into as a normal part of life in the city. You are never stranded. You never have to figure out how you are going to feed your family.

Bob: And this is part of what you mean when you say you feel a closer kinship with nature?

Mary: Yes, feeling part of nature because you depend on it more. Always before if it rained in the summertime, I might grow a pickle, but we didn't need the rain to sustain a garden. It was a respect for nature that we had never experienced before.

Bob: Had you thought you would gain this kind of respect before you moved here?

Mary: No, I think it really is just something that happened. We have always been outdoorsy to a certain extent with our vacations. But there, again, it was a more controlled environment, like stopping and looking at wildflowers, learning about trees, identifying birds, and that kind of thing. I had a rather romanticized feeling.

Bob: This has changed your philosophy about nature?

Mary: Yes, it has. I don't know many places in the United States that are still as wild as it is here. No one had lived here for ten years when we moved in. There are still some things I can't cope with. One thing is mice, which is ridiculous. After all I have done, I can't stand mice in the house! But, I killed a copperhead in the garden this summer. There was another snake in the chicken house that I had to kill. There are scorpions and tarantulas around, and this house was full of brown recluse spiders. There was one in the bathtub with the baby one day. I can now do things relatively calmly that nine months ago I could not handle.

Bob: Do you understand your own feelings better? Has that been affected?

Mary: Yes, I don't think we will ever look at things the same after having this experience. I think it has emphasized what we have always felt. We must take care of ourselves. In a philosophical way we have always felt people have got to learn how to survive. This just emphasizes it even more.

Bob: So many of your feelings are the same as when you came?

Mary: Yes. We have had a lot of romantic ideas busted. And I think if it were just Jim and me, we would have stayed. In fact, I'm sure we would.

Bob: How do the children make that much difference?

Mary: Well, there again I don't know how best to meet the situation we have, but we are blessed with very gifted children. Our oldest, who's in the fourth grade, was tested last year in Baltimore. She was placed in the gifted section. She is an extremely intelligent child, and it appears that our first grader is too. We thought that coming here would be a good educational experience for them. The schools in Baltimore are so involved in all the peripheral stuff in education. They always have so many specials and assemblies and little bits of planetarium and little bits of this and little bits of that. We didn't feel that this move would be a bad situation for them. We wanted a school without all the frills and extras. They could go to school and learn reading, writing, and arithmetic. We did not find that to be the case. Again, I don't know whether this is unique to this school or whether this is something that is experienced all over the Ozarks, but this school is just not equipped to deal with intelligent children. Class size is very small, but there are two classes per teacher. Everyone from the janitor to the cook to the principle is related. It is not an accredited grade school so they have limited federal money. They don't have the educational requirements for their teachers that they would have if they were an accredited school. I don't know that much about this kind of thing, but I do know that much. So they do not have a very good faculty. It is this attitude that we have experienced in the Ozarks of not wanting to change--not wanting anything that smacks of city. We've always done it this way! We're going to continue to do it this way! It's been adequate before, it will be adequate now! We have very purposely not gotten very involved in the school because we felt that we didn't want to push. But there are only eleven in our daughter's class, and five qualify for a learning disability class. So the intelligence level of children is pretty low here. They have rather antiquated text books. I remember using some of the same books as a child. Some of the information taught is erroneous. Our children have had very varied experiences. They have lived all over the country. They are interested in things that the children here don't seem to be interested in. In that way it was not a good situation for the children.

Bob: Is this what you expected?

Mary: No, not at all. This was not what we anticipated. We expected a very rural life with the children involved in raising animals. We thought it would be a good experience for them. We knew that at first they would not be able to fit in, but that the adjustment would take time. I think we had the feeling that the city was morally degrading. There was crime. Even in the suburbs you couldn't walk the streets at night, and the grade schools had drugs. We feared these things in the city. We had the mistaken idea that rural life was more wholesome--more what we were used to when we grew up. We did not find it to be so.

Drinking and fathers not working were the main things here. The kids were not interested in anything. Our kids were actually exposed to more vandalism and drunkenness here than they were in the city.

We had to pick up our kids after school at the store two miles from here. It is a liquor store and there is a pool room next to it. Almost every day there were men sitting in that store who were drunk or halfway there. You know, it just... The kids have learned to cope with it. I haven't. We took a load of neighborhood children to town once, and two of the girls were arguing about which building was the jail and how many times their daddies had been there. We just couldn't say we wanted our children to grow up in this kind of atmosphere. It sounds very elitist and I don't want to. But we didn't see that was any way to isolate our children and raise them in a good, clean farm atmosphere without being exposed to this.

A child wants to belong, and in order to belong he has to become like the majority. We feared that over the years, no matter what our influence, this would happen. They are intelligent and we wanted to give them many advantages--not advantages as much as opportunities to pursue whatever they wanted to pursue. We were shutting off some of those opportunities. It wasn't an atmosphere that we wanted. No, we chose it, but we had other opportunities. We wanted an education which we didn't feel they would get here. If we stayed, they wouldn't have those choices.

Bob: You couldn't have sent them to college if you had stayed?

Mary: No! Because of their intelligence they probably could have gotten a scholarship to go if they wanted to go. But, very few children who attended this school have ever gone to college. There is no emphasis on furthering your education. We found our children falling back. They were, for instance, coming home speaking incorrect English which they had never before done. They were developing attitudes we just didn't want them to have.

Bob: I don't get the feeling you think you have failed. You don't view it that way, do you?

Mary: No, not at all. I think that's important. If we were failing, we would have stayed. I know we would have because I can't think of anything we've every failed at. We'd just keep plugging away until we succeeded at it. We would stay if we were failing, definitely. But we knew we could make it. It just was not what we had hoped it would be.

This is comfortable to us. Here you are not trying to make impressions on anyone. People are very real here which is trite to say, but it's very true. People are basic. They don't really accept any kind of a front. We very much enjoyed the people we got to know. Every situation that we have been in has been a real experience for us and we have learned a great deal about it. I'm sure in six months we can look back and be a little more objective about it and some of the things we feel. But I think generally it has, as I said before, just confirmed for us what we thought.

Bob: What is Jim doing now?

Mary: He's back in the chemical industry and he is now a national marketing manager for a company in Kansas City. They have industrial chemicals. He is the national marketing manager for them all. He is basically in charge of about forty offices from the mid-west to the East Coast.

Bob: So he got kicked upstairs.

Mary: Really! It has been a good opportunity all around. He would not have been in a position to even be considered for this job if we had stayed in Baltimore. It really has worked out well. The reason we were surprised that it came so fast was that we were looking for a particular thing. We wanted to be in the west--no more East Coast. We wanted to be in a certain size city. We really had a lot of restrictions on what we wanted, but the fact that it came so quickly was a surprise. But we did find a place in Kansas City that is as far out as you can get. Although we only have an acre and one tree, we have a great garden spot and Jim can continue to raise his rabbits. Yet it is a good school system. We are hoping that we have found the best of both worlds.

Bob: What about this place? Have you sold it or will you sell it?

Mary: We haven't sold it yet, but we will. We're selling the house and half the land. Maybe it's because we don't want to give up or let go of the dream. You know, it was a dream for so long and it didn't work. And even though there was a lot of it that just wasn't right for us, it is still hard to give up.

Also, Jim and I kept thinking, 'the kids are going to adapt fine to going back but we 're going to have trouble again. We're going to be back in an urban situation. How are we going to relate again to our friends because our lifestyle is so different? How are we going to like having our neighbors on top of us again? What are they going to think of us raising rabbits in the back yard? So Jim and I are hanging on to this land thinking we will come back quite often and camp and spend our vacations here.

There are some side things I need to iron out--like in the hunger situation. How really do I feel about what's happening in that line? Unfortunately those who most need to know about nutrition do not necessarily have the background or the intelligence to comprehend what they need to do. I need to work that kind of thing through in my mind if I'm going to get back into it.

Bob: Do you think you will get back into it?

Mary: I feel sure I will because I've been involved in it, and I feel it is really important.

Bob: This would add tremendously to that interest.

Mary: Yes, I really feel it will. I feel like we sat in the city and collected clothes and gave food and money for food, but we never really knew what it was like to experience this kind of thing in our life. What are other people really looking for, if anything? I don't know whether this isolated experience of mine is true to any pattern. As I say, I know there are very good schools in this area. That's why I say it's unfortunate that if we had found a place elsewhere, this might not have happened.

Anyway, when our friends were saying, 'How can you leave this?' they meant how can you leave the hunting and fishing and beautiful air. These are people who maybe have a baby and that is all. Basically, we respond that we never had time to do things like that. We went fishing twice and never caught a fish. We never caught a fish here. With five of us in the family we didn't have time to go hunting. There was just never time to really enjoy the Ozarks. We thought we would be able to sit on the front porch and just soak it all in--fish every day if we wanted to. But, when our friends understood the decisions we were faced with, they really surprised me. They said that if they had the same opportunities we had, they would leave, too. I thought that was really interesting.

Bob: These are people who have lived here just a short time?

Mary: They've lived here a maximum of five or six years. And they love it and they love the lifestyle, and everything about it. But, if the struggle to survive were taken away, if they no longer had to struggle and it meant leaving here, they would leave. It was something I didn't expect because everyone who comes down here loves it. But, we are one of the few who could get out if we so decided. For most there is not that choice.

Bob: Certainly not as easily as you have done.

Mary: Correct, and not with the variation in income. They could be moving out of it, but not with the drastic increase in income that we are going to have.

Another thing we felt when we had been here six months was that the decision to leave would always get harder. We felt that we were going to slide so far into poverty that we would never get out or we would be forced to leave.

Bob: You thought the decision through very carefully?

Mary: Yes. Well, on the surface I'm sure it seems like it was a very quick decision. All of a sudden we were here and then, all of a sudden, we were gone. Some people must have thought it was a failure and that it was a fast decision. I suppose that time-wise it was a fast decision but it was a very well thought out one. The lowering of our economic level was not an unwelcome struggle.

Bob: Why?

Mary: Money has always come so easily and we never really spent it. It was a good feeling to have to work so hard to put food on the table. And, I think it was good for the children to say, 'now we cannot afford that,' or, 'let's make this,' rather than go out and buy it.

Bob: Do you see yourself as a social pioneer? Did you ever think of that?

Mary: I would hope so! I can't see very many people doing this, but I hope that everyone makes an attempt to at least know how to survive. People should grow a garden, raise something, and gain the satisfaction not only of doing it but also knowing that if the economy falls apart they can make it. I'm not one of these doomsayers, but, I guess going back to the hunger thing, I would like for more people to become conscious of what food means. I don't know how they can become personally conscious of it unless they experience something like this. But I doubt that will ever happen.

My experience has told me that for people who come here the lack of money is more of a challenge than a burden. For example, some new neighbors just mentioned the other day, 'We gave up soda pop to come here and we gave up...' It was a feeling of pride. They wanted to make it as a family with team effort. We are going to make it and struggle through this together.

Bob: The challenge becomes significant?

Mary: Yes.

Bob: And you knew what you were willing to give up to do it?

Mary: Yes, and we were very willing to trade off. The children were, too. We knew what we gave up which made the pleasures of growing everything and making everything even more so.

Bob: So it was a success every time you sat down at the table. You had accomplished something, hadn't you?

Mary: Yes, and I think it's that way for most people. In fact, when we get together socially, much of the conversation centers around things we've made. It's all very much wrapped up in doing or reading how to do things. There is very little talk of buying anything.

Bob: And that's accomplishment?

Mary: Yes, it's a whole attitude of buying or making. It's much better to make a hive for the bees than to buy one. It is the attitude that 'I'm going to make the best,' not 'Buy the best.' It is all a reverse of what we are hit with by the T.V. and in every aspect of our lives outside of these situations. You are looked up to if you have bought the best rather than if you made it.

Bob: A form of self-expression?

Mary: Yes, yes. Really. Jim made a furnace for this house out of two barrels. It would not impress our friends from the city that Jim made this wood furnace rather than buying the best furnace on the market. Maybe that's the big difference between us and our friends. They would not come out here and be impressed. To them the furnace would be two old barrels crudely put together.

Bob: But you did it on your own.

Mary: Yes. Yes. And it works.

Bob: And each cold morning you have to go down in that basement and put wood...

Mary: Right! Right!

Author's note--Some of Mary's comments about the school system and neighborhood are far from complimentary. I personally was acquainted with both the store and the school she talked about. Her description of the store was accurate. However, soon after she moved, new owners obtained the store and the clientele changed drastically. The store became a place where neighbors enjoyed meeting and shopping. Mary's description of the school, while probably exaggerated, is essentially correct. The school has continued to lose pupils and the tax base has also probably eroded. Nevertheless, there are excellent school systems in the rural Ozarks. Many high school graduates leave them well prepared for vocations or for pursuing education at higher levels.

CHAPTER IX

ONE WHO REMAINED

This is the story of a craftsman who has lived in the Ozarks for fifteen years. His experience is unique because of his hermit-like period. He intentionally withdrew into nature and himself. His withdrawal was more pronounced than anyone else I know. Yet, his insights, too, were sharper and clearer. Today he has reestablished his own gallery in the Ozark Mountains.

Bob: How did you happen to move to the Ozarks?

Darrel: I was living in New Mexico. I had already started as a worker in iron. I wanted to find a place in the country and live out in the woods--some kind of wilderness. I was visiting some friends in Oregon. In fact I almost bought a place just a few miles from the ocean, a real nice place that was 5 acres for $15,000.00. While I was visiting my friends I discovered that their folks had just found and bought a place out of a Strout catalog. I had never heard of a Strout catalog. We went to a nearby town and hunted a Strout office and got some catalogs. We got a big stack which included all of the last year's. We went through all of those catalogs and circled everything that sounded interesting wherever it was across the United States. Then we called them all. That was 25 or 30 places. Basically we wanted significant acreage and low price. Of all of the places we called, the one here was the only one that was on the market. I had never been to Missouri before we drove up to look at this piece of land. I couldn't believe it. I was born and raised in Southern Florida and at that time was living in New Mexico. I had spent all of my life except for my service career in warmer climates so it was pretty jungly to me. The forest were thick, but the place we looked at was 160 acres for $8,800.00. It was at the end of a road, and you had to drive through another person's property to get to it. There were a couple of old shacks on it and a spring that ran all year long that had some pools in it. It was exactly what I was looking for. It was perfect. I was looking for a location where I could be away from people more than anything else. The lady I was married to at the time was teaching school. I had a small gallery in New Mexico. We signed the contract, bought a pickup truck, and moved.

Bob: Why did you want to be away from people? It seems to be a significant criterion.

Darrel: It was the main thing--not just to be away from people but to be in nature. I didn't want to be away from people in a bombed out city. I wanted to be in the bosom of nature, you might say. That's something that had always been with me. In fact, after I lived here seven or eight years, I realized that what I was doing was precisely the dream that I had when I was six years old--the thing that I wanted even as a child was to be away from other people on land with water and animals. The world of humanity had always been a very strange place for me. It had always been ugly, busy, and unreal. Although I grew up in Florida, we were near some foothills so most of my spare time was spent in the hills. It was just a half mile walk to the brush. There were deer, mountain lions, and coyotes right there. Where the houses stopped, the coyotes and bobcats took over. I spent a lot of time with my family at an old family homestead. For me, it was always a sane place, a place that left clear, nice, refreshing, nourishing impressions, which were never there for me in the world of humanity.

Bob: Was this a difficult decision to make? You were married at the time.

Darrel: It was more difficult for my wife. Although she had grown up in the country in New Mexico, she never thought she would ever live so far back in the woods. Now I realize that it was not as far back in the woods as I thought it was. We didn't have running water. I still don't have running water, in-house plumbing, or that stuff--even after 15 years. She never got used to that. We carried water from the spring.

Bob: Leaving was not a problem for you or for her either?

Darrel: No, part of it was we weren't getting along all that well. It was a fresh start. It was one of those things. We had met in college. Marriage was formalizing an adolescent sexual relationship kind of thing.

Bob: How old were you at the time?

Darrel: I was 25. It was 15 years ago. Had been out of college a few years. Spent four years in the service, couple of years in school. I hated college. It was just better than working. Then I started working with the torch and doing some sculpture.

Bob: Were you making a good living then, financially? I assume you were?

Darrel: My wife had a teaching job, and New Mexico pays its teachers quite well. One of the best.

Bob: So you had a substantial income between the two of you?

Darrel: For me moving here meant a change from having a gallery to having no income whatsoever. For my wife it was the loss of a $12,000.00 a year teaching job--just a staggering amount. Fortunately she got a teaching job here immediately. But then things were different 15 years ago. There weren't that many people. There was a need for teachers. Now there are people standing in line for teaching positions around here. But in those days there were few outsiders in the area. Most of the people that lived around here were born and raised around here.

Bob: Describe your work, what you did then, or what you do.

Darrel: In those days, I was making bonsai and ecabena studies. Ecabena is flower arranging kinds of things, and the bonsai of course are trees. I got started in it when I set out to make a Christmas present for my mother one year. I used the equipment in the metal work shop in the art department when they didn't have classes going. I really enjoyed it and liked the way the little tree came out. I just kept doing it. Some of the interior design instructors said 'you could sell those things.' So, I found some interest and did sell several and that is how after tinkering with it for several years, I got started. One year I just didn't get around to going back to college. My wife and I were married. She had a pretty good teaching job. I opened the little gallery and started working. Then when we moved here, I just devoted myself to fixing the house up. There were two old shacks on the place that were very, very rough. They hadn't been lived in for decades, and needed a lot of everything. So I worked on the houses. I didn't worry about making a living. We didn't need a lot of money. We just didn't worry about it. Of course, I had my equipment set up in the other house. There were two old houses. I understand one was an old schoolhouse.

Finally I put some work together and started looking for some shows and started in making a living again.

Bob: You kept it together from then on.

Darrel: Yes, but the interesting thing was that there was no real market in the area then. Before the move I had stayed in the gallery. And now, things are different again. There are all kinds of tourist things, although that is not really what I do. My work is out of the major tourist business. But in those days I did a lot of things that were tourist items. Jim Matin had a shop nearby. I got associated with him. Max and all those people were looking for outlets. I found out about some shows from them, started doing some, and started traveling a great deal. Eight years later I got tired doing shows. I would be in Winter Park, Florida one month and then the next month I would be in Minneapolis. Then the next month I would be in Orangeberg, South Carolina, the next week Dallas. Those were good shows. It was easier to get into the good shows then because they had not been discovered economically at the time. The good shows, the best of the good shows, were the ones that it just made sense to do. In doing shows, you find there are regional artists. These are people who only do regional shows. If you do shows in a certain region, you will see the same people at those shows. Then there are some people who show nationally. I would see the same fellow in Winter Park and Detroit for instance. But if I did Detroit, Lansing and Grand Rapids I would see the same local craftsmen at those shows, too. It was an interesting subculture, an interesting way to make a living. But it was like a toggle switch. When the fun was over, I just couldn't stand it.

Bob: Was it a lucrative thing to do?

Darrel: Yes, but by then I was a bachelor. My work had always changed. So, I started doing trees. I did trees for many years. Then I started making fountains. Fountains were bigger, more expensive, and sold better. So eventually it got around to the point where my show was just fountains. It was just extraordinary, just far beyond anything I had imagined. But of course, I took it all for granted at the time. I had no idea I was doing so well. I made more money then than I do now, really.

Bob: But that really wasn't why you did it?

Darrel: I did it because I could sit down in my place and work undisturbed. I was having a heavy case of idealism in those days. It was not a particularly constructive time. A lot of things that I thought were bad were not necessarily bad. I went so far that all I ate came right out of the woods. All the meat and stuff like that. Just completely. I raised a little garden. But I would pick wild greens and then grow squash and potatoes and things like that. I would buy bulk grains, rice, beans, and things like that.

Bob: This went on for years?

Darrel: Yes, many, many years.

Bob: What did you learn?

Darrel: I learned that you can't turn your back on the world. There are all different points of view where you think, well now if I could just create this kind of circumstance, everything would be all right. I just wanted to turn my back on the world and leave it behind.

Bob: How often would you come out?

Darrel: Sometimes I wouldn't come out for over a month.

Bob: You saw no one?

Darrel: Oh, some friends or acquaintances would come down, that sort of thing. But I didn't need to come out. If I was down there a month and a half, I felt very pleased and exhilarated at not having gone out for that long.

Bob: Pleased in the sense of what?

Darrel: That I had managed to stay away from all of that nonsense for a whole month and a half. I didn't even have to go up to the highway. Craziness of the automobiles, cars.

Bob: Automobiles are still nonsense?

Darrel: Well, transportation is one thing. But of course every automobile is not just transportation. It is style, line, and form, and people's feelings about themselves. A car is like a Rorschach, just like clothing, just people inevitably expressing themselves. You cannot do other than express yourself with your vehicle, even if it is the most proletarian, practical, simple vehicle. It is an expression of your state of mind. If it is a Mercedes, it means you have a Mercedes set of head gear.

Bob: It is built into our culture?

Darrel: Oh, it is built into the organism. An Indian with a pinto pony is no different. The same phenomena is found on a different level in the most primitive aboriginal people. It is not a thing of culture. It is a thing of humanity. That thing of reenforcement, identity.

Bob: Surely we learn it?

Darrel: We learn how to express it. For instance, it is just like the hand; the mind has a shape and an organic structure, a genetic structure that is just as inviolate and unchanging as the hand. You can train your hands to do all different kinds of things. But the hand and the thumb are going to move the same way. It is going to grab the hammer in the same way. It doesn't make any difference if it is a carpenter with a hammer in his hand or an aborigine with a rock tied on a stick. He is going to hold it the same way because that is the way the body is built. Well, the attitude of the aborigine about his beaded moccasin is going to be the same as the attitude of the Texas oilman about his alligator cowboy boots because that is the way the mind is made.

Bob: Let's pull this back to the way you were living.

Darrel: Everything looked real ugly to me. There was no relief anywhere. Even the things I was making looked ugly to me, although I knew they were not. So imagine all of those ideas and attitudes in the mind of a person who makes pretty things and sells them. Why do people buy pretty things? Because they want them. They don't need them. They don't do anything. They can't eat them. So, of course, it was pretty, but you have to do something with it.

Bob: Didn't you feel a dichotomy with this? Wasn't there a lot of conflict?

Darrel: Oh yes, especially with the fountains. The trees I felt good about because I thought that it was a way of bringing a piece of nature into the home. I would find a rock that had a real wonderful landscape and feeling to it. It would have some moss on it and a beautiful weathered shape so that it was a beautiful rock. Then I would build the tree to enhance the rock, really. I created the tree to make the person aware of the rock, although the best of the trees were really nice objects too. I had good feelings about them because I thought an awareness of nature was missing from this culture. I thought people had lost touch with the organic world. So I always had a missionary zeal with the trees. I felt that I was bringing that feeling and experience into the lives of others.

Bob: So you switched to the fountains?

Darrel: I was seduced by the money. What can I say?

Bob: So you just kept making fountains while you had this conflict?

Darrel: So, eventually I couldn't stand it. I began making utilitarian things. I said to myself, "Here I am working with iron. I'll make utilitarian things. I'll make dust pans, candle holders, lamps, hall trees, kitchen utensil racks, and kerosene lights." Remember I had no electricity during all of those years, either. So I had a generator that I would fire up if I needed to drill a hole in a rock or something. So I made utilitarian things and started doing those same shows with the utilitarian things. Of course, my income plummeted because those things weren't quite as popular as the fountains. You can sell a few dust pans but not very many. It was very, very interesting.

Bob: Let's talk some more about what you were learning during that period.

Darrel: As I said, one thing I learned was that I couldn't turn my back on the world. The first thing I found out was the further I tried to bury myself the more the world was always there. I managed to get the land paid for. But when I had that land I suddenly had something to lose. I had taxes. With a chain saw, I had to have gasoline. When I cut my food down to where all I purchased from a store was grain, I still had to get the grain. There are all the transactions of making things. I still had to get the iron some place. I even had an acetylene generator in those days and made my own acetylene, but I still had to buy the carbide.

Bob: There is no way to avoid it.

Darrel: Exactly, so the more I tried to bury myself, the more I realized it was impossible, utterly impossible. I simply could not. I tried to resolve the problem. For instance my mind went to the most idealistic place I knew. I thought, "Well, I guess we could move to Alaska," and I even drove up to Alaska and looked around. It was a beautiful drive. Some places it is 170 miles between gas stations and there is not a side road or any building of any kind between those two gas stations. It gave me a whole different attitude about man's impact on the planet. So anyway I drove up there and looked around. But even up there it was obvious that I still couldn't get away from others and that I was falling deeper and deeper into an idealistic fantasy. Eventually I came to the conclusion that my whole attitude was an idealistic fantasy and that it was unobtainable and so I abandoned it. I recognized a responsibility to the planet. The idealistic fantasy is that I was saying to hell with culture. Culture is rotten and mankind is rotten. But you can't clean something up if you won't touch it. You have to be involved. So, I began seeing through the fantasy and the idealism. It changed everything. I saw that even the fountains weren't so bad.

Bob: Was this a fairly smooth transition? I assume it was a major transition in your life.

Darrel: Well, there were major points in it. Even before we moved here I spent years studying what is real. Then, I spent time overseas in the service. Some of it was in Europe and a couple of years in Asia, northern Japan and Korea, and a year in Vietnam. All of those experiences left me with a complete inability to be an American, or anything else. In Korean there are nine miles of road between the base and the town of Koonsong, and every building between the two locations is built of rice straw. The houses are thatched, chicken coops are thatched, and the fences are thatched. The military paved the road between the two and the very first year the Koreans tore the road up and burned it for fuel. Then, in Vietnam I saw people starving in the streets, literally starving, skin and bones looking through straw heaps for something to eat. It was horribly demoralizing. Then, at the same time I witnessed the wonderful kindness of the Japanese people and the Koreans. They were so kind. And the United States is such a gifted part of the world with such awesomely gifted people.

Bob: Would you explain that, please?

Darrel: The United States is rich in resources, intelligence, and opportunity. No other place in the world exists with the kind of opportunity we have in the United States. Literally still to this day someone who grows up around here could conceivably be President.

Bob: Nowhere else in the world?

Darrel: Not that I've ever seen. Certainly not in Japan or other places in the East. And not in Germany or France. There is a greater sense of class consciousness there. We have a much more liberal attitude in regards to social class consciousness. In other countries the thing that keeps a man from humble roots from becoming politically important is class consciousness.

Bob: This was all weighing on you?

Darrel: Wondering! The things I saw had to make some kind of sense. There had to be a reason for the way things were and there had to be some sense to it. There had to be a purpose. Of course, you can find all kinds of people who will tell you what the purpose is, and you can find it in books and all of the rest of that. That's very nice for someone who can believe. But if, for whatever reason, you find yourself incapable of believing and the only thing that will do is the real, then, until you have drunk in the spring, all of the dissertations on the taste of water won't satisfy that thirst.

Bob: Let's talk about the fact that you are a craftsman. You make things; you create things; you have since high school.

Darrel: Actually, I have made my living at it for seventeen years.

Bob: It is important to you to make things isn't it? To create things?

Darrel: Yes. But not necessarily out of metal.

Bob: Let's talk about the act of creation. What is it to create. You do create don't you?

Darrel: You know there are some schools of thought in anthropology which believe that man is a maker of things and that is what sets him apart from other animals. Now, other animals do make things. Birds weave nests and ants make hills, but man has such incredible powers of synthesis and creation that he is like unto the Creator. The image of the Creator, at least, is inventive intelligence, creative synthesis, and energy.

Bob: That is a part of what you are?

Darrel: It is a part of everyone. Everyone creates. A person operating a machine lathe or a cash register in a grocery store is using his creative energy. The same thing applies to a person who teaches school.

Bob: But some people are certainly more creative than others. For some people it is creative to sit on an assembly line but that also thwarts an awful lot of...

Darrel: I separate participatory from generative creativity. The guy on the assembly line putting on lug nuts all day long is participating in someone else's creativity. If you view all of life as creativity, then everyone is creating equally. No one is more or less creative than another. But, an assembly line worker is not generating creation, he is participating in creation. That is probably the demarcation between artistry and craftsmanship. The craftsman is being creative but is not generating creativity.

The artist is generating. He is exploring new frontiers, strolling through the jungle. "Look Mom, no hands."

Bob: But some people are more adept at this. It seems to be part and parcel of some people.

Darrel Oh, absolutely! I think a great deal of that has to do with genetic structure, early experiences, and how much anxiety a person can put up with. A lot of people say, "Oh gosh, if I could only do thus and so." But what keeps them from doing thus and so is their anxiety. The only way a person gets to be an artist or a craftsman is either to be born into the household of an artist or craftsman so he is free from anxieties, or else have the inner qualities that permit him to survive and overcome his anxieties about not being plugged into the "system". The artist is just as plugged in as everyone else. He just doesn't know it when he begins. Everyone has to start from scratch.

Bob: They have to be plugged in in their own way.

Darrel: Exactly.

Bob: Many of the people coming here, I believe, were searching for a different way to get plugged in.

Darrel: Wholesome, I think, is a good word. I think people come here looking for a more wholesome way of being, not just a way of living, but of a way of being.

Bob: Let's keep this to you and your experience. Did this happen to you, the words you are using now? After you were here for a number of years were you a more wholesome person?

Darrel: Absolutely. I don't know if I am a wholesome person, but I think I got healed. I suppose that is real close. In fact, I think if there is any genuine accomplishment in the work I am doing now it utterly has to do with the experience of living here. It is as necessary for me to have close contact with nature as it is to have food and air. The quiet and the opportunity to work, to question, and to look in solitude helped heal me. I had sensitivity poisoning or something. I was not able to give because I needed too much. For one thing, I wasn't able to give to society because I didn't want to give them anything anyway. People looked ugly to me then.

Bob: You find a need, or a responsibility at least, to interact with others now, don't you? To let them know what you have learned?

Darrel: My goal for my work now is to show people unexpected vistas within themselves. Within the last four or five years the work has been getting to where I feel good about it. Craft shows are becoming like laboratories, giant laboratories where I can take the objects and all these people walk by and experience the objects. It stops them for a moment. They experience the object, the lines, the sense of balance, the form, the colors, the textures--all of those things produce an experience for them that is actually them. They are experiencing themselves but have given the object credit for having produced the qualities. Actually they possess the qualities, the object just showed them how to be in that shape, how to be in that way.

Bob: Whether it is beautiful, quaint, interesting?

Darrel: Yes, yes.

Bob: Let's take that back to where we were a few moments ago. Many people are moving into this area and they are coming in for a lot of reasons. Some want jobs, money, to retire. There are lots of reasons. But some are moving in so that they can significantly change their lifestyles. They want major changes in the quality of their lives. Would you agree that this is an act of creation?

Darrel: The changing lifestyle? Yes, the most creative thing a person can do. Everything you create is a reflection of your state of being. So creating a state of being creates your creation. The people who move for the specific reason of receiving a different category of impressions in their day to day lives and a different quality of being, would be involved in an extraordinary act of creation. That would probably be the most, or at least one of the most, significant creative acts that a human being could perform.

Bob: It would be important for that person to be an artist in some way?

Darrel: Of course! Those are the people who want to grow a garden or cut their own wood because to them the creativeness of it is where the nourishment is.

Bob: Exactly. They want to work in leather, copper, become woodworkers or something like that.

Darrel: That is why you see so many craftsman in this area. There really are an inordinate number of craftsmen in this area, but many of them sell their goods outside the area.

Bob: Why do all of these people live here then?

Darrel: It is wonderful. For one thing I think it is the lay of the land. For instance in California or any place in the West where you have those vast dramatic vistas, 40 acres is just a little sloped spot on a giant hillside. But here 40 acres has its own little hills and hollows and warmth and a sense of intimacy.

Bob: So this is just...

Darrel: It is custom made...

Bob: Inspiring or energizing, is that the word?

Darrel: Perhaps. See the west coast country is what I call inspiring. But here nourishing is a real good word.

Bob: Yes, I think that would fit. So you see other people moving here seeking this kind of nourishment.

Darrel: Another thing about the Ozarks is that land used to be cheap, but now it is very quickly becoming high-priced. Those people who generate creativity will look at the price of inexpensive land and its ability to nourish and will immediately want to move here. They want some of it. Those who use their creativity to pay bills, meet deadlines, and keep their jobs,--it is a way for them to ward off their anxiety--will not make the move.

Bob: Could you have stayed in New Mexico and changed as an individual? Could other people stay in the urban area and make the same kinds of changes?

Darrel: I don't think so. The urban area would not have tolerated it. To change, a person must be open and that makes a person vulnerable. Part of the thing that is so wonderful about the

Ozarks is the degree of vulnerability that is permitted. People are genuinely friendly here. People are not cold to each other. They are not indifferent. There is certainly no animosity around here. The whole countryside is like a small town in terms of rumors, and everybody knows everything.

But the quality of the impressions, what you see, and the vulnerability, for instance, in the suburbs has something to do with a man-created world. Everything in the suburbs is created by man. If a tree exists, it is because a man set it there. It is a different kind of impression. The person who has developed a taste for nature is also vulnerable to the ugly as well as the beautiful. You can't shut out the ugly and receive the beautiful. If you want the beauty, you have to take it all.

Bob: Once you make the shift then you begin to move to a difference cadence. You redefine yourself in relationship to this new environment.

Darrel: Often a value system is characterized by vulnerability. If all you see is concrete jungle...

Bob: Buildings, streets, and traffic jams.

Darrel: If you are vulnerable to that in an aesthetic way...

Bob: You've got to move on.

Darrel: Exactly.

Bob: The best place you are going to move is where you are going to survive inexpensively...

Darrel: Find some land...

Bob: And find the support you are going to get. The culture of the Ozarks is...

Darrel: Custom made. Yes.

Bob: But it seems to me that if we are talking about people who live in the suburbs and are not reacting to much other than the cadence of the machines that are in the city, they would be anxious to move. Why wouldn't they readily choose this alternative?

Darrel: You see, an alternative is not available if you are bound by your appetites and your fears.

Bob: You've got to proceed.

Darrel: It takes three things to make the decision to change: capacity, perception, and will. Fear can thwart all of these. Fear colors our perceptions, dampens our capacities, and weakens our will. Fear is one of the reasons people trade their creative existence for standing in front of a machine lathe eight hours a day. They are afraid of what will happen if they don't. How are they going to feed their families, put clothes on their backs, and care for their kids? That is very real anxiety.

Bob: That is important to most people.

Darrel: It is important to everybody because those things have to be taken care of. Even the saints had to make a living. This is interesting because it brings us full circle to the folks who have migrated to the Ozarks; and migration is probably a good word, because it means that those people have the capacity, the perception and the will.

Bob: A while ago we were talking about people who moved from many other areas, but they sure didn't know each other before they arrived.

Darrel: Yes

Bob: And somehow the same force existed in each place that pressured them or prompted them to choose to leave.

Darrel: There is repulsion and retraction both.

Bob: There was another force that pulled them at the same time?

Darrel: Yes.

Bob: It has to be a cultural force.

Darrel: Absolutely.

Bob: Beyond the simply personal level?

Darrel: The interesting thing is that most of the first immigrants didn't know anybody here. In fact, few of my friends who have moved here in the past few years had friends or acquaintances here when they arrived. I had never been to Missouri before. Most of those people had just passed through. One fellow that I know who was a very successful Boston artist just left Boston. He had a beautiful gallery just outside Boston. In fact he has work in the Metropolitan Museum of Modern Art and years ago was written up in Newsweek and Time. He bought a used delivery van, loaded his family in it, and headed off with no destination. He went to New York, to the Carolina's, and through Tennessee. He ended up in the Ozarks. Some of the more esoteric types will say there is an Atlantean crystal buried in the Ozarks that is attracting folks. However you want to slice it up, the interesting thing is that even the people who are that far out recognize that there is something here.

Bob: Something attracts them.

Darrel: It is unquestionably true.

Bob: There is a myth of self-sufficiency in the culture, and in many ways the culture lives up to its myth--the old traditional.

Darrel: You mean the Ozark culture?

Bob: Hard work, hard play, independent action.

Darrel: Self reliance.

Bob: Mutual interdependence.

Darrel: Self reliance, because if you don't have people who are self reliant, you can't have mutual interdependence.

Bob: That's right and they go together.

Darrel: Exactly.

Bob: They are not mutually exclusive.

Darrel: Exactly.

Bob: If you are self reliant...

Darrel: Then you have something to give. If you are not self reliant, you have nothing to give.

Bob: You have to have something beyond yourself. Trade or barter, share, give of yourself, or whatever. Man is not an island.

Darrel: Certainly not. The man who thinks he is, is a starry-eyed idealist and is a dangerous force to others because receptive young minds will listen to that and say, "Oh, that sounds wonderful."

Bob: The process that you went through is a sorting out of priorities; establishing what is important and what is not; what used to be important and what still is.

Darrel: Priorities! I would say priorities are accidental to values. It is one's values that establish priorities. What changes are not a person's priorities but a person's values, and a change of value is a change of being.

Bob: And the way we express them.

Darrel: Inevitably. It will involve itself in expression. Our values simply will be expressed from the soles of our feet to what is written on the baseball cap on our head. See, even the food on the table expresses our values.

Bob: But what about the guy in the city who wants to move here. Perhaps he finds that he cannot express his values at least to his own satisfaction, or...

Darrel: Or that he is living in a value system that does not reflect his own.

Bob: And the values of the city are so incompatible with his own that he's got to load his family into a rental truck and say "We are going to find a place that is more mutually acceptable."

Darrel: I know some people who recently moved here from Mason City. The husband has always been a cabinet maker. They don't want to do a lot. They make their living with their hands, making things, doing whatever for whoever. He does wonderful work, but he doesn't want to make a lot of money. He just wants to make his land payment and put food on the table.

Bob: It has to do with simplifying a lifestyle.

Darrel: Yes, very much so. Larry is going through an interesting transition. He is just beginning to see that you can't get away. He came to the Ozarks to get away and now is discovering that you can't get away. He is looking at his thinking again and beginning to restructure. A new reality is just beginning to emerge. You can see where its dim light is starting.

Bob: There seems to be a pattern to this. It is a good change for people who take the time to go through it, I think. I am assuming that many people want to, but only a few decide to make the change. Those who move are the tip of the iceberg of those who want to.

Darrel: There are those who tantalize themselves.

Bob: Yes, there are a few who come and that's what we see.

Darrel: But what keeps the rest from coming but anxiety? What is the energy of all of the evil in the world but anxiety?

Bob: I never heard of it that way before...

Darrel: The very absence of anxiety is love.

Bob: I look at the process of coming here as a very creative process, anybody who does that...

Darrel: I agree.

Bob: Your statement... What is the essence of creativity?

Darrel: Create anew--to actively participate in the creation of oneself--to take the reins!

Chapter X

CONCLUSIONS

When I first became interested in this subject some of my friends were very pointed in their comments. "Who were these people that I was interviewing?" they asked. Wasn't it obvious that they were "drop-outs from society," "hippies left over from the sixties," or perhaps merely deviates who had no other choices? No normal self-respecting American, some of them blatantly stated, volunteered to receive less rather than more money unless they were without a choice to do so. As surely as the little old lady from Pasadena cannot play for the Boston Celtics, so these who had so spontaneously appeared in the Ozarks could not survive in an industrial society. They were the urban drop-outs of the '70's and '80's, people who could not cope, could not make it where they were, and whose only hope of surviving was in a rural environment. They were a new class of "hanger-ons."

My first responses, based in social thought, were to defend the migrants. There is a theory in sociology which states that when any mass migration occurs, whether that migration occurred because Europeans exited to the United states in the late 1800's, blacks to the cities in the '50's and '60's, or urban dwellers to the sun belt of the '60's and '70's,--it is always the smartest, wealthiest, and best educated who first discern the opportunity and reach for the advantages. The theory states that the insightful and opportunistic always lead the way.

Was this also true of the migration to the Ozarks? It was difficult to determine who was moving and the motives behind their decisions. At the beginning I turned to the whirring computers at the University Library in Columbia, Missouri to help with a literature search. I watched in amazement as a young lady told me of the many hundreds of thousands of references stored in computers across the nation which were available to her instantly by telephone. In a matter of minutes she had tapped into several of them. But for all of her effort she could only find two or three references which were even related to the topic. No help apparent there. At that time few demographers had studied the movement. There was no money to run a sophisticated and statistically correct random sample "Harris Poll" survey. Nor did the decadal census offer much insight into the population shift. The census barely kept track of who moved--it certainly did not register their former places of residence, and in no way counted those whose move was accompanied by a voluntary lowering of income. The traditional sources of demographic information were of little help.

My interest was specific. I was concerned with people who had lowered their income when they moved. I thought that their decisions ran contrary to the decisions which most people make. What, I wanted to know, prompted them to make these decisions? Were they the forerunners of a larger movement yet to come? Have many become so disenchanted with the urban areas that they prefer to leave them for simpler surroundings?

There were some things I was aware of. My major association with contacts for the study came through my office at the University of Missouri Extension Office in Galena, Missouri. As an outreach center of the University, our task was to disseminate information and answer questions which related to agriculture, youth work, 4-H clubs, home economics, and public affairs. It was the kind of information which people new to the

Ozarks were desirous of obtaining. Almost to a person, everyone in this study has in some way been in contact with a University Extension Office. Many came to our office seeking assistance and on a few occasions ended up working for us, serving on advisory boards, or volunteering to help with an educational project we were promoting.

While I was well aware that this was a non-scientific sample of the area's populace, I knew that those who came into the office--and those who talked so spontaneously in interviews--were a cross-section of society. There were former mechanics, laboratory assistants, school teachers, factory workers, construction workers, executives, and social workers. Some had high school educations--some did not. A few held college degrees. Some had been wealthy--most had not. No, the theory of the brightest and the best, in terms of wealth and education, did not fit. And, as the floodgate opened and more and more moved in, it was obvious that they were necessarily more than urban drop-outs. Too many arrived, and their life stories were too coherent to be those of dysfunctional social deviants. The common denominator, if one existed, was lodged somewhere else in the gratings of culture.

My trips across the Ozarks left me with time to ponder the strengths, wisdom, and skills of those who moved. What were the trends in what they were doing? I concluded that they had to be extremely skillful to make such a move. Any common denominator would have to include the words sensitive and insightful as well as resourceful. Independent of each other they had made a similar decisions and shared similar hopes, dreams, and concerns. But their decisions were individually made. They could only support each other after the move.

The encompassing nature of the move has already been discussed in preceding chapters. People were concerned with living and did not want to find at the end of their lives that they had not lived well. It was not that they were preoccupied with morbid thoughts of death, although there were certainly discussion of serious illness, dying, and death. But with probably only one exception, they believed that they passed through life only once. They wanted to live as well as possible on that one trip around. Perhaps their viewpoint on retirement more than any other single subject portrayed their attitudes about living. Many talked of "doing it now instead of after retirement," "retirement will take care of itself," "our health might not allow us to do this after we retire," or "we're incorporating retirement into what we're doing now." Clearly living in such a way that they could share, love, and give, rather than be drained by the daily grind of life was the dream they embodied. When the end approached, each wanted to view his life as having been worth living.

There were surprises, too, during the course of the interviews. One was the extent to which the arts and crafts influenced the lives of those who moved. It was a rare person who had not mastered a new skill--including carpentry, gardening, leather crafts, cabinet making, crocheting, blacksmithing, and pottery. So basic to their lives were the arts and crafts that I ceased to ask if people had one, but rather asked what it was. Never did I have anything but a positive response to the question. A few developed the craft into a livelihood. But most used them as hobbies and devoted what time they could to creative expression. One man kept his leatherwork tools under his bed; another maintained his shop of woodworking tools should he ever need to return to cabinet making.

The arts and crafts helped supply an impetus to the move. When people first discovered they could work in a craft and creatively express themselves, they began to wonder if the same might also be true of their own lifestyles. They wondered if the knowledge, self assurance, and success which the arts and crafts fostered might not also transfer to their entire lives. It was an inauspicious beginning for such major consequences.

The one major theme which I came across that I totally did not anticipate was that of the relationship of personal change to the spiritual world. There was a near-universal reliance on religion. Even when I didn't ask about their spiritual lives, individuals volunteered that such beliefs had prompted or sustained them during their change. At first I was apprehensive at the reliance on God, religion, and the spiritual world and wanted to account for the events in social and psychological terms. And yet, the evidence mounted.

In an early interview a husband and wife told me they were Mennonites but could not worship in their church because none existed in the area. During the discussion the young father quietly left the room and returned beaming proudly and wearing a long black coat and top hat. He proudly identified the traditional clothes which his sect wore to worship services. He had a beard--and I envisioned a smiling Abe Lincoln in front of me as he and his wife discussed the beliefs of the Mennonites. This same intensity was reached again when a young Quaker mother related her experience of a dramatic conversion to a conservative "born again" Christian belief; another mother prayed daily although she seldom went to church; and a young man meditated by reading the lives of the Eastern mystics. Almost every family related a mystical experience to me. The importance of spiritual belief could not be denied.

Part of this emphasis on religion can be explained, I'm sure, by the fact that when people undergo significant changes in their lives, they often simultaneously experience confusion and frustration. Moving into the unknown is uncomfortable for most. They have a need for unity, certainty, and a central truth, a stable "rock of ages" on which to rely. Religion often supplies that permanence, as it did here, and people drew on it.

But the reliance on religion was more important than a temporary resting place. For many who moved spiritual growth was at the heart of their decisions. Spiritual growth was inseparable from their moving, growing, and changing. At first much of this change was into an area in which they had little understanding. The growth was nurtured from the unknown--from a mystical realm. It was fostered by the interest in the out-of-doors, interpersonal relations, and the expressive arts. This spiritual growth allowed people to divest themselves of material things and seek a higher order. It was compelling. I'm sure many considered their transition to be a spiritual odyssey.

Another common question I encountered was concerned with those who succeeded. How could a person know before or during the change if he was going to succeed? The question is a little like predicting the score of the Notre Dame-Michigan State football game in 1997. Obviously, the winner will be the team that has the best players, is well prepared, and then executes superbly. There were guidelines to success, but I could find no rules.

A simplified answer is that those who laid the best plans and worked the hardest succeeded. Plans needed to be carefully detailed--preferably years in advance. Family finances, which dominated the concerns of most people, needed to be worked out. People needed to pay for food, clothing, housing, and insurance. They could do with less, but they couldn't do without. I knew only two or three families who were able to live on what I considered meager possessions. One couple had built a one-room house, carried water from a near-by well, and were satisfied. Another raised a family on a small farm of rocky hillsides and cedar glades--a condition indicative of poor soil in the Ozarks. Both of these families spent many hours working. They were satisfied with their change, but they had little time to relax. Life was hard for them.

But hard work alone did not insure success. Personal needs and goals also had to be attended to. People could do with less money only when their activity had meaning. The potter could throw pots when he had a compelling need to create and was willing to trade less income for the freedom to express his creativity. Or, the people who gardened could raise produce for the family table rather than obtain a job in town, for they enjoyed the outdoors, the earth, communing with nature, and took great pride in eating what they had grown. Self-fulfillment was essential to success.

Most who moved wanted land ownership and ended up on small farms. They found living on the land an extremely satisfying endeavor. The gardening, raising animals, watching the seasons, believing oneself secure with property, and watching an investment were all a part of farm ownership. The work was difficult and any equipment purchased was expensive. It was, perhaps, the modern equivalent of forty acres and a mule.

Benefits of farm ownership were rarely economic in nature. Property and equipment costs were too high to recoup expenses in a short period of time. At a time when jobs were scarce and family finances always important, the farm often drained money rather than producing income. The farming was frequently subsidized with income gained by those employed off the farm. But many anticipated this problem even before making the move. For them the benefits of ownership far outstripped the disadvantages.

Recently this pattern of small farm ownership has been given a name by rural sociologists. They describe it as part of the two-tier farming establishment which has emerged in this country. One type is the huge farms, those comprising thousands of acres and hundreds of thousand or millions of dollars, and headed by giant corporations. The other is the very small farm--the size of the ones that have been created by those who have been moving to the Ozarks. The increase in these two farm sizes has been carved from the medium sized family farms which have dwindled in number until they face extinction.

One cannot help but wonder, though, if the small farms may not provide the stability for food production and become the basis for regional food production centers in the future. Certainly large farms have shown a recent vulnerability to national economic conditions. What will happen to them if recent trends continue or if difficult national economic conditions again appear? May not the reliance on food production switch to small farms and regional commerce? The ground work for this may be developing with local farmers' markets, small co-ops, and roadside stands. These emerging patterns, coupled with the resourcefulness of those who live on small farms, may develop as a national food reserve. In years ahead the public interest may be served by such efforts.

Another factor in success, too, was tenacity. To succeed it was necessary to want to succeed. Along the way some people encountered extremely difficult situations and overcame them with nothing less than heroic efforts. The story was included earlier of the couple who built their own house and lived for a winter in a small 10 x 20 room at the neighbors--then invested all their savings in the house. They then worked day and night to make their dream come true. Not included was another story of a fiercely proud man with several children who related how events had been so unexpected and damaging that one Christmas was joyfully celebrated because a few days earlier he and his family learned they had qualified for aid from the state welfare system. Only through such aid, he stated, could they have celebrated Christmas. It was one of the best Christmases they had ever celebrated. A few months passed and they no longer needed such help. But that Christmas was a demarcation point for them. Others talked about adversity, too. There were tales of unscrupulous realtors drastically overpricing land, of agricultural commodity markets drying up, and declining livestock prices. Factories closed shortly after employment was obtained. Divorce came unexpectedly. Everyone had problems. Still, people insisted they had changed their lifestyles for the better--life was simpler.

One of the major questions I posed to myself while traveling through the Ozarks was why should a person make a geographical move? I wondered why it wouldn't be better to attempt this personal change while remaining in the old neighborhood, keeping the same employment, allowing the children to attend the old school, and retaining as many friends as possible? If a person remained in an urban area and put as much effort into the change as he did once he had moved, couldn't he make at least as dramatic a change in his lifestyle with less disruption? Couldn't he avoid the geographical move if he so desired?

Many questions have no definitive answers. Surely this is one of them. The answer probably centers around the need for support from others. Decisions regarding income level, employment, housing, and friendships could have all been examined while remaining in an urban area. But the most long-lasting and probably difficult decisions were those that had to do with values, beliefs, ethics, and attitudes. It was the inward changes that required the most nurturing from friends, neighbors, and "kindred-souls" who shared a similar dream. But people found this support difficult to obtain.

Even before moving, people found they were becoming incompatible with neighbors, friends, and even relatives. Acquaintances, instead of being sympathetic and supporting allies, often became questioning, suspicious, and resentful antagonists. To many the urban climate became counterproductive. And support groups, which are so prevalent in society to help so many, have not developed for those who intentionally want to change their lifestyles. Groups exist to help alcoholics, the over-weight, divorcees, drug addicts, and AIDS victims. But little organized help exists for those desirous of simplifying their lives. Remaining and simultaneously changing became an almost impossible task. Those who made the decision to move had a faith that such support exists in the Ozarks. They believed they would find encouragement in the long-standing traditions of the native residents and in their association with others like themselves. The choice to move became increasingly enticing.

I suspect that there are many in the urban area who think about moving but do not. I've wondered why they don't. When people are individually contemplating a change of such magnitude, alone and without contact from others, the decision is an extremely difficult one. To leave other people, a job, and a lifestyle behind cannot be an easily made decision. Perhaps an even more fundamental reason to forestall a move is the answer I received from a friend after he had recently moved into the area. His response was that people often feel they have only one career, one home, one family, and one lifestyle within them. A change of such magnitude, he felt, required a total self examination. To examine so much was more than most people could readily handle. They preferred to forever delay making a decision.

Of those who move, who succeeds? What allows people to fit together all the diverse fragments necessary to change a lifestyle? How do people create a new future for themselves and still provide for their daily necessities? The answers seem clear. Those who have a strong vision of a new future based on a revitalization both of themselves and others find the endurance and create the renewal which allows them to celebrate their chosen task of remaking and extending themselves. They are willing to experiment both with themselves and society. Their visions are of a sustainable society in which people matter. It is one where people take control of their own lives and rely on themselves, friends, and neighbors for meeting most of their needs. Those who understand themselves and can be insightful without being critical are the ones who succeed. The change is a propelling force fostered from within.

FOOTNOTES

1. Daryl Hobbs, Evelyn Cleveland and Bill Elder. 1981. *Regional and Metropolitan Population Shifts in the U.S.1970-1980. Report #007.* Columbia, Missouri: Office of Social and Economic Data, University of Missouri.

2. Milton D. Rafferty. 1980. *The Ozarks: Land and Life.* Norman, Oklahoma: University of Oklahoma Press. Pp. 57-60.

3. Calvin Beale's analysis of the population shift has been most helpful. See Calvin Beale, "A Further Look at Nonmetropolitan Population Growth Since 1970." *American Journal of Agricultural Economics*, (December 1976).

4. Andrew J. Sofranko and James D. Williams. 1980. "Characteristics of Migrants and Residents". Pg. 22 in *Rebirth of Rural America: Rural Migration in the Midwest.* Ames, Iowa: North Central Regional Center for Rural Development.

BIBLIOGRAPHY: HELPFUL SOURCES

Berry, Wendell,

1978 *The Unsettling of America: Culture and Agriculture.* San Francisco: Sierra Club Books

Brownell, Baker

1950 *The Human Community.* New York: Harper and Brothers.

Elgin, Duane

1981 *Voluntary Simplicity.* New York: William Morrow and Company.

Gerlach, Russell L.

1976 *Immigrants in the Ozarks: A Study in Ethnic Geography.* Columbia, Missouri: University of Missouri Press.

Hays, Jack, ed.

1978 *Living on a Few Acres. Yearbook of Agriculture.* Washington: U. S. Government Printing Office.

The Mother Earth News.

n.d. Through its articles and interviews this popular magazine has had an inordinate influence on the shift back to the land.

Nearing, Helen and Scott

1970 *Living the Good Life.* New York: Schocken Books

Rafferty, Milton D.
1980 *The Ozarks: Land and Life.*
Norman, Oklahoma: University of Oklahoma Press.

Rodale Press, Emaus, Pa.
This press has been involved in publishing a variety of periodicals and books on organic gardening, agriculture, and back-to-the-land publications for many years. Their practical "how-to" approach has been helpful to many.

Schumacher, Ernest Friedrich
1979 *Good Works.*
New York: Harper Row
1977 *A Guide for the Perplexed.*
New York: Harper and Row.
1975 *Small is Beautiful: Economics as if People Mattered.*
New York: Harper and Row

Thoreau, Henry D.
1970 *The Annotated Walden: Walden; or, Life in the Woods.*
Edited. New York: C.N. Potter.

Wigginton, Eliot
1972-1980 *Foxfire, Vols. I-VIIII*
This six volume set of books on traditional "how-to" has spurred the interest of many by examining the technology of an earlier time

Many people are quoted in this book. The names and identifying backgrounds of those who were interviewed have been changed to protect their privacy. However, great care has been taken to quote accurately and place all comments in the context in which they were originally made.